Builder
Ministry
for the 21st Century

REV. DR. DAVID S. LUECKE

CONCORDIA PUBLISHING HOUSE · SAINT LOUIS

Published by Concordia Publishing House
3558 S. Jefferson Ave., St. Louis, MO 63118-3968
1-800-325-3040 • www.cph.org

Unless otherwise noted, Scripture quotations from the ESV Bible® (The Holy Bible, English Standard Version®), copyright ©2001 by Crossway Bibles, a publishing ministry of Good News Publishers. Used by permission. All rights reserved.

Scripture quotations marked NIV are taken from the Holy Bible, New International Version®. NIV®. Copyright © 1973, 1978, 1984 by International Bible Society. Used by permission of Zondervan Publishing House. All rights reserved.

Scripture quotations marked RSV are from the Revised Standard Version of the Bible, copyright 1952, © 1971 by the Division of Christian Education of the National Council of the Churches of Christ in the United States of America. Used by permission. All rights reserved.

Cover image © Shutterstock, Inc.

Manufactured in the United States of America

Library of Congress Cataloging-in-Publication Data

Luecke, David S., 1940-
  Builder ministry in the twenty-first century / David S. Luecke.
    p. cm.
  ISBN 978-0-7586-1669-2
  1. Church renewal--Lutheran Church. I. Title.
  BX8065.3.L84   2010
  254--dc22   2009045826

1 2 3 4 5 6 7 8 9 10   19 18 17 16 15 14 13 12 11 10

Contents

Introduction

This book is intended to promote productive discussion among ministers and church leaders who are concerned about the future of their congregations and church bodies.

In many parts of the country the context in which ministry is done has changed considerably in the last generation. A visual check on Sunday services shows many congregations with few young families and children. To be in a church is no longer as important to Americans as it was in the decades after the Second World War.

One set of pastors and church leaders seems resigned to the inevitableness of church decline driven by demographic changes. Since 1960 in the United States, Lutherans, Presbyterians, and Episcopalians combined have seen the proportion of their membership per 1,000 population shrink almost in half from 8.5% to 4.5%. Another set of leaders is looking for ways to alter the course. Sometimes the motivation seems to be to maintain institutional health. The best motivation, though, stays focused on the mission of connecting more people with Christ.

Chapter 1 notes how the overlap between a congregation's loyal church community and the larger social community is disappearing, especially in urban and suburban settings. It offers the distinction between churches whose doctrine leads them to baptize infants and those churches that baptize only those who can confess their belief. Believer-baptizing church bodies, frequently called Evangelicals, seem better able to fold new, unchurched people into their fellowship. Infant-baptizing church bodies, which are centuries old, have grown reliant on a loyal fellowship of members introduced into the fellowship and trained in its ways as children. They tend to take loyalty more for granted than Evangelical churches do. At issue is not the doctrine of the Sacrament of Baptism. The focus is on its social implications for community building.

Another key distinction is between a shepherd model of ministry and a builder model. The shepherd model is beloved and has worked well for centuries. It keys off of Jesus' command to Peter to feed his sheep. As will be developed, the Apostle Paul worked more with a builder model, stressing building up the fellowship as the body of Christ. Building up involves movement and change. Churches with a tradition that emphasizes shepherding but which are no longer thriving would do well to consider a more builder style of ministry.

Chapter 2 shows how churches that stayed with their roots in European state-protected church bodies have a valuable heritage of stressing the objective truths about God, sin, Christ, and salvation. But they have also acquired resistance to stressing how Biblical doctrine can become subjective in the hearts and feelings of members. Such churches respond well to issues of *faithfulness*. Their heritage does not equip them well to address issues of *fruitfulness*.

The bottom-line message of this book is that Lutherans, Episcopalians, and Presbyterians need to become better at promoting and sharing personal spiritual experiences. Instead of "assuming the spiritual goods" of life in Christ, they need to be more effective at "delivering the spiritual goods."

Chapter 3 focuses on the inherited shepherd model of ministry, with its strengths and weaknesses. It demonstrates how its precondition of having a loyal membership is declining in many geographic areas of America. With such decline comes less fruitfulness.

Chapter 4 describes the builder model of ministry that is oriented to building up the fellowship of Christ's body in a particular location. A builder by trade, the Apostle Paul used a special vocabulary to stress how his ministry revolved around building up in as many ways as he could the relationships with Christ and with each other in His body. For Paul, church was all about the changes of moving toward more Christ-likeness in personal and congregational life.

Chapter 5 presents the fellowship builder's box of tools. None are new. But suggestions are made for how they can be re-focused and practiced when the objective is to build up a fellowship of Christ's body today. This is a one-chapter **Part II**.

Part III presents ways to Build More Fruitful Relationships in a congregation.

Chapter 6 discusses how to cultivate the soil for the Holy Spirit's work in a congregation. We often forget or overlook the truth that it is the Spirit who calls, gathers, enlightens, and sanctifies the whole Christian church on earth. Our human efforts are necessary, but sufficiency for growth comes only by the Spirit. For Paul the challenge is to make good use of gifts given by the Spirit to every member to contribute something to the common good.

Chapter 7 explores the place of personal spiritual experience and feelings in church life together. Paul recognized feelings as fruit of the Holy Spirit, who can transform lives. Feelings shaped by the Spirit are to be considered good and faithful. Feelings of guilt are declining in their ability to motivate involvement in church activities.

Chapter 8 highlights how church bodies develop their own customs and cultures for living out their faith. These become traditions. They consist of approaches toward, among other things, presenting and receiving truths of the Bible, for praying, for making music, for raising children. Seldom is it wise or even possible to change a whole culture. But trying out new techniques here and there may help overcome a cultural weakness.

Part IV addresses how to lead the processes for helping a congregation become more responsive to the changed context for ministry today.

Chapter 9 is entitled *Organizing to Build Up the Fellowship*. It distinguishes between a congregation's formal organization in service to its basic identity as an informal fellowship. Church organizations can and should be changing to better address issues important to the health of its fellowship and to remain more responsive to the Holy Spirit. Leaders can be more focused in these efforts by recognizing and strengthening eight qualities of a congregation, as worked out in Natural Church Development.

Chapter 10 develops the role of oversight in church leadership. The English translation of "overseer" is bishop. Good overseers offer both structure and support for workers. Paul distinguished between supervisors (bishops) and helpers (deacons), and urged the principle of entrusting what he said to reliable people who will teach it to others. The builder model calls for raising up and training many helper-leaders.

The final chapter, **Chapter 11**, focuses on the transition process. When change is defined as happening in the context of an activity, transition describes how an individual or a congregation adjusts to that change. The transition process has four predictable phases. In guiding transitions, leaders need to keep the church focused on goals beyond its own self-interests and to work hard to avoid serious conflict. Some analytical tools for that purpose are described.

Concluding thoughts suggests the proper relationships between faithfulness and fruitfulness:

Full faithfulness brings lasting fruitfulness.

Lasting fruitfulness depends on full faithfulness.

TWO EMPHASES FOR MINISTRY TODAY

The chart on the following page presents the basic two models that will be discussed in this book. They both focus on a specific congregation and its "one another" relationships with Christ and among participants.

These models can also be considered paradigms for two different emphases in ministry. A paradigm in today's use describes a set of assumptions about what needs to be done and the appropriate ways to do that.

The shepherd model and the builder model are not mutually exclusive. Good ministry involves both outlooks. But individual ministers will usually tend more in one direction than the other.

The shepherd model tends to fit best in the geographic and social context of congregations in rural areas and small towns. The builder model tends to fit best the context for ministry in larger metropolitan areas.

The right side model summarizes the shepherd minister's assumption about and emphases on how to *Apply* God's Word, what the *Focus* for these efforts should be, what *Accents* will be given, and who does the *Ministry*.

The left side model summarizes the builder minister's assumptions about and emphases on how to *Apply* God's Word, what the *Focus* for these efforts should be, what *Accents* will be given, and who does the *Ministry*.

Two Paradigms to Guide Ministry Today

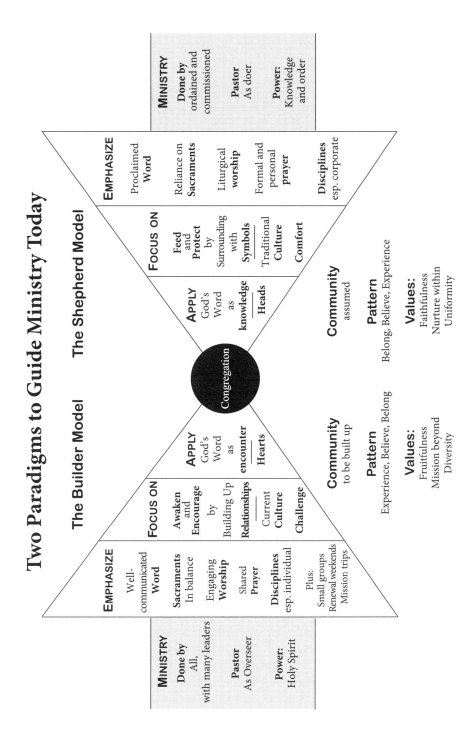

The Builder Model   **The Shepherd Model**

MINISTRY
Done by ordained and commissioned

Pastor
As doer

Power:
Knowledge and order

EMPHASIZE
Proclaimed Word

Reliance on **Sacraments**

Liturgical **worship**

Formal and personal **prayer**

Disciplines
esp. corporate

FOCUS ON

Feed and Protect by Surrounding with **Symbols**

Traditional **Culture**

Comfort

APPLY
God's Word as knowledge
Heads

Congregation

Community
assumed

Pattern
Belong, Believe, Experience

Values:
Faithfulness
Nurture within
Uniformity

APPLY
God's Word as encounter
Hearts

FOCUS ON

Awaken and Encourage by Building Up **Relationships**

Current **Culture**

Challenge

EMPHASIZE
Well-communicated **Word**

Sacraments
In balance

Engaging **Worship**

Shared **Prayer**

Disciplines
esp. individual

Plus:
Small groups
Renewal weekends
Mission trips

MINISTRY
Done by All, with many leaders

Pastor
As Overseer

Power:
Holy Spirit

Community
to be built up

Pattern
Experience, Believe, Belong

Values:
Fruitfulness
Mission beyond
Diversity

7

1

The Shepherd and Builder Models for Ministry

Pastoring a congregation is harder than it was in the past.

That's the starting assumption of this book. Identifying the problems of today is the basic task. Pointing toward solutions is the aim.

Christian ministry has always been hard. So many different expectations have to be met. Not the least of these is interpreting God's intentions for a particular congregation. Dealing with conflict has been an ever-present source of stress. For many generations ministry meant living in poverty.

Yet today ministry is harder.

The vitality of so many congregations is seeping away. Members are aging and graying. Children's Sunday School in so many churches is a fraction of what it used to be. Growth was the general expectation for ministers through the 1960s and 70s; if not in their congregation, then in someone else's in the denomination. Now good ministry too often amounts to slowing down the rate of decline. Decline saps energy and confidence.

Facing hard times puts churches in line with many other institutions in America today. The dynamics at work are the same that Michael Barone identifies in his stimulating discussion of *Hard America, Soft America* (2004).[1]

HARD AMERICA

Barone documents how new forms of competition are forcing a sorting out in business, the military, and government agencies. Cheaper goods from abroad put price pressures on American manufacturers, leading to downsizing and sending jobs offshore. With no draft and an ongoing war, military forces have to adopt new ways to attract recruits and retain veterans; the new Army has been forced to change its traditional ways.

Churches face the same social forces today: more competition and higher expectations. More competition comes not only in the form of neighboring churches with more program offerings, more sophisticated communication, and better facilities, but also in the presence of many more alternative ways to spend Sunday mornings. Higher expectations turn into loss of loyalty and greater readiness to go someplace else when "this church doesn't meet my needs." Christian churches in America had grown used to depending on loyalty to sustain membership and ministries. There is much less tolerance now for poor performance, especially with worship and sermons that fall short of engaging the participants.

Many Christian churches are used to functioning in a "soft" environment where a sense of church identity is strong and performance expectations are often low. Their heritage comes from European state churches, which more or less guaranteed funding. In this country until the last half century, most congregations were in villages and small towns where community was strong and competition light.

The problem with such churches in hard America today, though, is that fewer new participants show up and membership dwindles. There is usually no safety net, because denominational resources are also dwindling. At least one Protestant church body anticipates that about one third of its congregations will wither away and die in the next fifteen years.

LESS HARD FOR SOME—CHURCHES WITH OVERLAPPING COMMUNITIES

Some churches today are still able to carry on their ministries in a relatively soft environment. Rural and small-town congregations usually can count on loyalty and "normal" competition; there is a high overlap between the congregational community and the stable, larger social community. Any decline in church membership can usually be attributed to general rural population decline.

The hardened environment affects especially suburban churches, where the competition is greatest. Discussions of aggressive, cutting-edge ministries often leave small-town ministers and churches perplexed and defensive. What they are doing is still good enough, and the need for change is less apparent. In many Protestant church bodies today, up to half the congregations are rural or small town. Yet they make up only a quarter or third of the membership in the denomination. Their viewpoint brings resistance to change by colleagues whose suburban context has in fact become much harder.

The future for churches that are slow to adapt can be seen in empty buildings of inner-city urban congregations. When those who built up these congregations moved on, few of the new residents of old neighborhoods found their way to the remaining ministries, even when the church carried out well-intended mission outreach. The history of inner-city churches can make apparent that congregations and church bodies have distinct cultures which can become mismatched with the expectations of new residents from other cultural backgrounds. The question then is, How much can and should a church change its inherited culture to appeal to new people?

HARDER FOR SOME OTHERS: SUBURBAN INFANT-BAPTIZING CHURCHES

We can recognize two kinds of Protestant church bodies. Some have had almost their whole history in the American experience. Baptists and Pentecostals are the most visible examples. Others brought with them and still value their European heritage, such as Episcopalians, Presbyterians, and Lutherans. Increasingly their need is to develop new ways and to devote more energy to bring new people into Christian community.

Churches in the first group are often described as Evangelical. Church bodies in the second group were known as "mainline" churches, because in fact until recent decades they were the most visible and largest Protestant church bodies; now the term "old line" is in use.

A very unsettling, well-known fact of American life is that mainline church bodies have been in a period of decline in membership and influence for the last four decades. Since 1960 Episcopalian and United Church of Christ memberships have declined by about a third; Presbyterians and Methodists by about one quarter. Where there is growth in churches, it is usually among Evangelicals, many of which identify themselves simply as community churches. Since 1960 Southern Baptists added two-thirds more members and Assemblies of God increased fourfold.[2] While considered "mainline," Methodist and United Church of Christ will not be included in following discussions because their agenda does not value their European heritage as highly as do Lutherans, Presbyterians, and Episcopalians.

American-based church bodies have more experience building up the community life of a congregation and seem better able to reach out and integrate people from different backgrounds. Carrying little social legacy from Europe, they early on had to develop new techniques and to devote more energy to building relationships in Christian community than did the European-oriented bodies that could more readily assume a preexisting community for their church life.

FAITHFUL AND FRUITFUL

The basic problem of old-line churches is that their inherited ways of thinking about church and ministry did not much pursue questions of performance or fruitfulness—what makes one congregation better than another. More specifically, what fruits should be expected of a Christian church and how can they be assessed? Withering congregations, like withering plants, call fruitfulness into question.

Old European-oriented church traditions offer few generally accepted answers to *fruitfulness*. The central value was *faithfulness* to the church or governing body and its doctrinal standards. Their organizations were structured mostly to deal with conflict, not effectiveness. This was possible because those congregations could take existence of a functioning community for granted or its development was plausible. Opinions about what makes one congregation better than another are certainly widely held. The issue is whether those answers remain faithful to the defining identity of the church body.

THE SHEPHERD AND BUILDER MODELS FOR MINISTRY

Pastor David Schaefer's congregation numbers about 400 baptized. As he looks at his schedule for the coming week, he sees that he has two Bible classes to teach as well as two sermons to prepare because this is Lent. He has to make three hospital calls, and one of them will probably turn into a funeral this week. He is scheduled for at least two shut-in calls and he really ought to visit several families he has not seen for a while. He thinks about the members who have made an appointment this week to seek his pastoral counsel. Thursday evening is the monthly council meeting, and he has to work out the agenda. Tuesday is an elder's meeting he needs to attend. The ladies group wants him to do a short devotion at their meeting Tuesday morning. Pastor Schaefer is very busy. Pastor Schaefer is a shepherd minister.

Pastor Paul Baumann also serves a congregation of about 400. He is looking forward to the Wednesday evening Lenten service for which a woman of the congregation has prepared a series of dramas for him to base his message on. He needs to refer two hospital calls to Mary, who does a great job with her ministry of visitation. Three small groups are meeting for Bible study and prayer; he met with the leaders last week. He looks forward to the Thursday afternoon planning meeting with the church's part-time music director to work out the worship emphases for the month after Easter. Maybe Friday he will arrange to have lunch with the church's youth leader at his workplace. His lunch today is to help the council chairman work out the agenda for Thursday evening's meeting. Pastor Baumann thrives on involving members in multiplying ministries of the congregation. Pastor Baumann is a builder minister.

What is a shepherd minister and what is a builder minister? These two vignettes are meant to illustrate that the two ministers really go about their work differently. One tends to do all the acts of ministry himself. The other tends to raise up other doers and leaders to help with ministry to others. A good builder minister will certainly at times act as a faithful shepherd, caring for individuals and protecting the members from false teachings. The question is whether faithful shepherds, when necessary, can also function as builders working through others.

Shepherds and builders are not mutually exclusive. Good ministry involves both outlooks. An instinctive builder minister usually does not need to be reminded to act as a shepherd for certain purposes. The thrust of this book is to challenge shepherds in metropolitan areas to stretch themselves also into builder perspectives.

The two approaches will be summarized in the chart that appears later in this chapter, which becomes a guide for development in later chapters. These are two different models—two ways to organize one's thinking about roles, emphases, and tasks of ministry.

"Paradigm" has become a popular word to describe a set of assumptions about what needs to be done and the customary ways of doing that. In the face of major social change, the set of assumptions basic to shepherd ministry often are no longer well-grounded, and in those situations, customary approaches to church life often no longer bring effectiveness as well as they did in earlier generations. In those circumstances, a new set of assumptions may help highlight new emphases in ministry. Thus the builder paradigm will be contrasted to the traditional shepherd outlook.

One assumption of this analysis must be very clearly recognized: Where shepherd conditions still exist and where shepherd ministry still supports healthy and lively congregational life, there may be little need to change. As will be developed, these situations tend to be in rural areas and small towns, where a sense of social community is still strong. The builder paradigm, on the other hand, is meant for situations where traditional ministry no longer brings exemplary and sustainable church life for a congregation. These conditions tend to be in large metropolitan areas.

In the New Testament, it is Jesus who is the Good Shepherd, and that metaphor is beloved, especially as expressed in Psalm 23. Jesus uses it to reinstate Peter after his betrayal. The exchange in John 21 is very moving. Three times Jesus asks Peter if he loves Him. Three times Peter says, of course. Three times Jesus says, then feed and take care of My sheep.

But Jesus also used the building metaphor. In an earlier exchange with Peter, whose name means rock, Jesus acknowledged Peter's confession of Him as the Messiah and then said, "You are Peter, and on this rock I will build My church" (Matthew 16:18).

Implicitly Jesus acknowledges that shepherd is a good image for ministry relationships to individuals, but builder is a more fitting image for binding individuals together in church. Jesus taught the Kingdom of God as heartfelt relationships with God and between individuals; he did not found the institutionalized church. As he said to Peter, he left this task to his disciples. The apostles wrestled with how to turn the vision of Kingdom relationships into congregations that grew and sustained themselves over the years. The builder is a better analogy for that purpose.

Paul made heavy usage of it. He saw himself as a builder, indeed, the master builder (1 Corinthians 3:10). He used builder vocabulary extensively. His choice of the root Greek word in its noun and verb forms appears thirty-two times, as will be developed in chapter 4.

The term *shepherd* appears only twice in reference to Paul: Ephesians 4:11 ("shepherds coupled to teachers") and Acts 20:27 ("be shepherds of the church of God"). When in 1 Corinthians 12:28 Paul repeats the Ephesians listing, he eliminates shepherd and just mentions teachers. In Acts we may be dealing with Luke's recollection of Paul. In Paul's own writings, there is only that one Ephesians occurrence. The same phrase about being shepherds also appears in Peter's only usage of the shepherd image (1 Peter 5:2). Like Paul, Peter also developed the builder analogy, in his earlier chapter (2:4–7).

It's amazing that over the centuries, Christian church leaders did not pick up on the builder image to guide their work. Much of the explanation can be found in the predominantly rural nature of old church bodies. That was certainly true in Europe, where before 1800 about 90 percent of the population lived in the country. At the end of the nineteenth century in the United States, 65 percent of the population was rural and small town. Now that proportion is only 25 percent. Rural analogies were a natural for ministry up to and well into the twentieth century.

But much more significant was the reality of stability. Families grew up on the farm and expected to spend their whole life there. Congregations were made up mostly of lifetime members. A church was a flock to be fed and protected. Most area residents would identify themselves as Christian, and appealing beyond the membership was sheep stealing. Ministry could be relatively easy.

So much has changed in the last half century. Freed from the land, people move around much more. Familiar relationships get left behind. There are many indicators, discussed in chapter 3, of how a strong sense of community is being lost in America today. Life becomes a process of building new relationships. "To build a relationship" is the phrase so often used. Some churches are better able to do that than others.

Almost all of the two thousand year history of the Christian church in the West has been lived out in times of stable community. How different that is from the world faced by the apostles. In the roughly 150 years before Christ and through the apostles' generation, the Roman military built and kept safe the extensive road system that connected the far-flung, large metropolitan areas of the Roman Empire. The history and writings of the apostles reflect how extensive travel could be. The roads and their safety declined rapidly with the collapse of the Empire, and mobility stayed very limited through the Middle Ages and Reformation. More than ever we now face what the apostles faced—a highly mobile, urban-based population basically hostile to the Christian message and morality. What many churches deal with today looks more like Corinth, Ephesus, and Rome than the Wittenberg, Westminster, or Canterbury settings that shaped the heritage of ministry carried on by churches that still value their European roots.

It is time to learn new lessons from the apostles. It is time to pay more attention to how they went about building congregations.

The shepherd image will always be important for Christian ministry. It carries forward important values for pastoral relationships. But it can be supplemented by the builder image. This is not an issue of *either* shepherd *or* builder but rather getting more adept at *both* shepherd *and* builder.

In modern physics, wave theory and quantum theory offer differing explanations for the properties of light. Which you use depends on what you are trying to accomplish. So can it be with models of ministry.

TWO PARADIGMS TO GUIDE MINISTRY TODAY

The following chart contrasts, in a hyperbolized way, how the shepherd approach and the builder approach conceptualize the ministry task and emphases as well as the ministers' own identity. At the bottom of the chart are underlying assumptions for each model that will be very important to understand. Ministry, in practice, will usually have a blend of each but will tend more in one direction than the other.

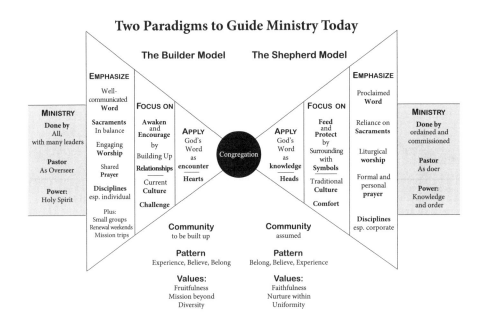

Two Paradigms to Guide Ministry Today

HOW SHEPHERDS SEE MINISTRY TASKS, EMPHASES, AND IDENTITY

To appreciate shepherd ministry at its best, think of a village in Saxony in the nineteenth century or a very small town in Iowa in the early twentieth century. The people are tied to the land through their farms; they expect to be there for life. Everybody knows almost everybody else; they shop together, send their children to the same school, and solve community problems together. They know each other's foibles and are quite conscious of what others think of them. The sense of community is strong and includes gentle pressures to be like everyone else.

In the shepherd model, the basic ministry task is to guide through life the flock gathered in that area, the members in the geographic parish. Their church gives them identity, and their loyalty is expected. The minister feeds and protects. This is done by surrounding them repeatedly and as much as possible with God's truth conveyed through sermons, lessons, worship forms, and visible symbols as well as baptisms, weddings, and funerals. The intent is to extend and deepen participants' understanding of life with God in all its richness. This becomes a matter of reminding them of who they are. The care of souls offers the comfort of God's love in crises.

The shepherd model emphasizes the proclamation of God's Word. This is the primary responsibility of the pastor. The relevance and importance of God's Word in the inspired words of Scripture is a given; the need is to make fresh application. Preaching is based on the lectionary, the assigned readings for the week. The sacraments can be powerful sources of comfort for those who rightly understand them, and considerable time is devoted to teaching and celebrating them. Formalized liturgical worship best conveys the richness of God's truth and presence, and repetition is good. Formal, written prayers are highly valued, and participants are encouraged to do any additional prayer alone in their own personal prayer life.

The shepherd model of ministry features an established congregation with a minister ordained on the basis of special education. Conventionally this pastor does all the important Word ministries of preaching, teaching, leading worship, and pastoral care. Others help with secondary, support work. The shepherd model features a two-part distinction within churches: the clergy and everyone else, called laity.

HOW BUILDERS SEE MINISTRY TASKS, EMPHASES, AND IDENTITY

A builder of physical structures brings change to lumber, bricks, and pipes by connecting them to make something greater than the parts.

The ministry builder's task is to expand and build up people's connections with Christ and with each other. Ministry is all about relationships. Supplemental to God's truth as symbol, like doctrine, is God's truth as encounter and experience. The appeal is as much to hearts as it is to heads. Awakening and encouraging new experiences are tasks added to feeding and protecting. Challenge is in a steady rhythm with comfort.

The builder model revolves around making new connections. The Word of God is to be communicated, not just proclaimed. Keeping the attention of the hearers and addressing their perceived needs is a high priority. This often means topical preaching using a variety of communication techniques. The sacraments are valued, but no more than the well-communicated Word. Worship needs to engage the participants; informality, simplicity, and more familiar musical expressions are seen as better ways to do this. Informal prayer shared among participants helps build relationships.

The builder model focuses on expanding relationships, often beyond the congregation. All the members, as the priesthood of all believers, are seen as the ministers, adding their service to that of others and multiplying Christ-focused relationships. The ordained ministers oversee this ministry done by many.

This model has a threefold distinction between the ordained, the participants, and helper-leader ministry staff in between. The more the helpers can support other participants in their ministries, the better.

CONTRASTING VALUES

Where the *shepherd* would highly value faithfulness to tradition because it has worked so well in the past, the *builder* focuses on effectiveness or fruitfulness—what is working now. The *shepherd* places high value on nurture within the fellowship; the *builder* is looking for new connections beyond as well as within the congregation. *Shepherd*s value uniformity in patterns and practices of church life. *Builders* bless diversity that better fits the needs and expectations of those with whom they are trying to make new connections.

CONTRASTING PATTERNS FOR CHURCH LIFE

The pattern of development that works so well in the parish ministry of a shepherd starts with the assumption of belonging; participants are born into the congregation through infant baptism. Then the challenge is to help them learn to believe what the fellowship believes; for children this is done with confirmation. Whether or not the participants have a strong heartfelt experience with God is a low priority; more important is living out the shared identity of the flock, the gathered family of God.

Instead of working with the pattern of Belonging leading to Believing and maybe to Experiencing, the church bodies that have been most effective in America work with the opposite pattern: Experiencing, Believing, Belonging. Such ministry helps participants experience God's presence in their lives, teaches them what to believe about this relationship, and then encourages them to become part of the fellowship.

In this pattern, being born again into Christian faith is the starting point for a believer, and this has to happen when the individual is old enough to understand the experience, which is expected to happen at a specific time and place. Telling your "born-again story" provides entrance into a church fellowship. The fastest-growing expression of Christianity around the world is in Pentecostal forms that stress emotional experiences of the Holy Spirit. Being born of the Spirit is often considered a second spiritual rebirth. Worship services are usually emotionally charged. From no presence in 1900, Pentecostal churches are reported now to have 523 million adherents worldwide, second in Christianity only to Roman Catholicism.[3]

Churches that value their European heritage as an established church body almost all practice infant baptism. Almost all churches whose heritage is from the American experience practice believer baptism. These two different heritages with their different theologies lead to congregational cultures with differing expectations for the minister. The shepherd is at home in infant-baptizing churches. The builder, to date, is more likely to be found in believer-baptizing congregations.

CONTRASTING PERSPECTIVES ON PERSONAL SPIRITUAL EXPERIENCE

As the opposite progressions point out, a key difference between ministry as a shepherd or as a builder is the emphasis on personal experience. The feeding and protecting *shepherd* in a stable community need not expect that members will have a decisive, memorable personal encounter with God. In fact, anyone acting out a special emotional, very high level of conviction can be unwelcome as disruptive to the many without such an experience. This happened in thousands of congregations during the charismatic movement of the 1960s and 70s.

The *builder* welcomes personal subjective experiences and aims to help such experiences happen. They become important connecting points. Key to a person being drawn to God and a specific congregation is experiencing satisfaction of needs he or she is aware of. In a village, satisfaction and fulfillment are not important concepts. They are in suburbs with high turnover and lots of competition.

Guilt is a powerful motivator in a small established community for people ready to let their church identity be a firm statement of who they are. Traditionally *shepherd* ministers can use it as an effective motivator for participating in church life. In large sprawling communities of the twenty-first century, however, guilt does not work well anymore. Few neighbors know each other. Churchgoers are a minority among the many unchurched and de-churched around them. They participate because involvement fills a need, not because of concern what others will think about them. *Builders* are need oriented.

These contrasts between the shepherd model and the builder model are summarized in the chart presented earlier. Both models point to the congregation, the basic unit of church where Christian faith, life, and witness are worked out. Each model has its own understanding of how to apply God's Word, what the basic tasks are, and what should be emphasized. Driving each model are differing concepts of what ministry is and who does it. The contrasts of specific columns will be discussed in subsequent chapters. The outside columns for each model are highlighted and developed in chapter 10.

QUESTIONS FOR DISCUSSION

1. Is ministry in a Protestant congregation harder today than it was in the past?
2. Is the geographic community of your congregation stable or with high turnover?
3. What is your reaction to the initial distinctions between shepherd and builder ministry?
4. Does the suggested contrast in patterns of involvement square with your impressions?
5. How important is it for church members to have personal religious experiences?

2

Truth, Faith and the Holy Spirit

Their approach to personal spiritual experience is one of the basic distinctions between shepherd and builder ministers. The tradition emphasizes the sequence of Belonging (through infant baptism), Believing (through confirmation) and then maybe Experiencing spiritual awakenings. Growing believer-baptizing churches emphasize the opposite sequence for involvement in church life: Experiencing (through conversion), Believing (confession of faith at baptism) and then Belonging to a local congregation—maybe. With this opposite approach, loyalty to a congregation or church body is usually not as high as found in church bodies that celebrate their European heritage.

These two different sequences express differing assumptions about God's truth, the nature of faith, and the work of the Holy Spirit. These are heavy topics that merit attention.

The role of personal spiritual experiences in Christian life can become clearer by distinguishing between objective truth and subjective truth, between faith as knowledge and faith as encounter.

Objective truth is the content of faith, expressed as teachings of the church, that is, correct doctrine. Getting the doctrine wrong might lead members astray. That is why in shepherd congregations, the professional, ordained minister should do all of the preaching, teaching, worship leading and pastoral care. Having the Word of God preached and taught serves as a symbol of what holds the congregation together. Whether that Word is preached and applied well or poorly is not crucial to the flock. They will return out of loyalty. Shepherd ministers are used to appealing to heads more than hearts. Emotions are a by-product. Yet even though these are usually below the surface, strong emotions of loyalty are often present. Just try to change a village church and you will see compelling feelings of barely concealed anger emerge in resistance.

The word for faith in Scripture has two meanings. One is the content of belief, true teachings about God. The other is the act of trusting the God who is confessed. The first is objective truth, truth beyond me. The second is subjective truth, truth for me and within me.

TRUTH

As the content of belief, objective truth is the whole range of doctrines that a church body teaches: God the Father as creator, human sinfulness, Jesus Christ as true God and true man who is the only way to salvation, God the Holy Spirit who brings spiritual life by way of Word and Sacraments through churches as the body of Christ.

The intent in the present writing is to be doctrinally orthodox throughout. What questions are raised will be in the specialized understanding of church and ministry.

Truth becomes subjective as convictions and emotions get attached to it. How that happens is a serious theological issue with important implications for ministry. Ultimately God is the one who moves head knowledge into the heart through the Holy Spirit. The person cannot take credit. Godly convictions and emotions are the consequences of God's movement, not the cause. That relationship is clarified in this comment by a mature Christian, "At the time I thought I was making the decision to accept Christ. But looking back on it, I now realize it was all by God's grace."

Yet the Holy Spirit's job is harder with people who are not catching the message and do not understand in their own frame of reference the meaning of God's saving love. The way objective truth is presented makes a difference in how it becomes subjective truth for specific individuals.

FAITH

It is easier to preach and teach objective truth as the faith confessed in the doctrinal content of the written, inspired Word of God. It is more difficult to recognize and facilitate subjective truth, that is, faith as an act of trust in the God presented by the written Word. This faith is the personal relationship a believer has with God.

Luther's term for this trust was *Christ for me*. His whole life was a response, and he expected personal responses from those he preached to and taught. Certainly faith as an act of trust in God always needs to be based on what we know about the God of Scripture. But this objective truth has not completed its God-given task until there is a personal response of trust.

THE HOLY SPIRIT

What is abundantly clear is that the Holy Spirit is basic to the process by which objective truth becomes a subjective response of individuals. Orthodox Protestant theology of the Reformers teaches this. The Holy Spirit is God's counselor, or advocate, to the individual. Jesus teaches in John 3:5–8 that to enter the kingdom of God one must be born again, or more specifically, born from above by the Holy Spirit. The Apostle Paul taught the Corinthians that no one can say Jesus is Lord without the Holy Spirit.

Yet church bodies with very long traditions are cautious about what to expect from the Spirit in routine church life. The rest of Jesus' teaching about the Holy Spirit is very difficult to handle, for "the wind blows wherever it pleases. You hear its sound but you cannot tell where it comes from or where it is going. So it is with everyone born of the Spirit."

Unpredictable congregational life in a village parish is hard on everybody, not just the minister. Someone who has had an intense personal spiritual experience can be intimidating to "normal" Christians. Those with spiritual responsibility are rightfully concerned lest such individuals justify their unusual behavior with the claim that it came from the Holy Spirit and then insist that all others should have the same encounter. Conflict is almost inevitable, and this is bad, because historically those in the village have nowhere else to go. So wise and appropriate teaching is that the trustworthy Holy Spirit comes only through means, especially that of Scripture as the Word of God. The power for congregational life comes by handling those means carefully. Through them come clear biblical knowledge and preservation of good order.

Renewing an appreciation for the work of the Holy Spirit in church life is basic to developing a fruitful building ministry. The Spirit provides the best power for church life. Reformation teachings about the Spirit, especially as presented by Martin Luther, are much richer than what was filtered through the traditions inherited in early twentieth-century church life. Luther's two Pentecost hymns "Come, Holy Ghost, God and Lord" and "To God the Holy Spirit Let Us Pray" are vibrant with anticipation of fervent love and hearts set ablaze with sacred fire that the Holy Spirit brings.

In the Lutheran heritage, two key biblical teachings about the Spirit received little attention. One is Paul's teaching on the *gifts of the Holy Spirit* in Romans 12 and 1 Corinthians 12. The Spirit prompts individual members to contribute to the congregation what they enjoy and do well, offering such gifts as proclaiming, teaching, caring, contributing finances, and doing administration. These then become the basic building blocks for a builder ministry. Engaging the spiritually gifted produces a fundamentally different dynamic for congregational life than found in a traditional shepherd ministry. Paul's teaching on gifts of the spirit will be developed in chapter 6.

The other focuses on Paul's teaching in Galatians 5:22, 23 about the *fruit of the Spirit*: love, joy, hope, patience, kindness, goodness, faithfulness, gentleness and self-control. Those are not just abstract concepts. They can and should be emotions that become life-directing personal experiences, and they can become so when the work of the Holy Spirit is carefully cultivated in church life. Such emotions will be developed in chapter 7.

TOO FAR

Subjective truth is objective truth that becomes personal. Can an emphasis on personal spiritual experiences go too far? Certainly. Established traditions are primed to prevent that.

But can an emphasis on *objective truth* go too far? This question is usually not asked in long-established church traditions. It is the question that opens up issues of fruitfulness.

TOO OBJECTIVE

Emphasis on objective truth can go too far when truth is wrapped in vocabulary and practices that are not readily accessible to people not already established in that church community.

A simple example can be found in ethnic churches in America. Their native language can work well for the first generation and maybe the second. But they usually figure out that if they want to hold the third generation, they had better switch to language and forms more accessible for their grandchildren. Few average new residents moving into a community would think of checking out their local Greek Orthodox church. They would readily assume it is not for people like them. How many would have similar reservations about their local Lutheran church with its German or Scandinavian background? Even when the language is English, traditional doctrinal teaching is expressed with many Greek- and Latin-derived words that carry less meaning to newer generations that were not taught Latin in high school.

When the biblical truths of Scripture come wrapped not only in language but also in forms that are hard to comprehend and appreciate, the Holy Spirit is less able to touch their hearts. Minimal fruitfulness in congregational life could be a symptom that ministry has gone too far in the objective direction.

The worship tensions of the last several decades are an expression of different emphases on subjective or objective truth. Traditional forms have been cultivated to have an other-worldly feel about them—to be objective. Organ music, layers of floor-length vestments, well-crafted prayers in classical English with scripted responses are meant to be different from everyday life. They portray the transcendent God.

In comparison, contemporary expressions usually aim to produce music, language and forms closer to everyday experience. They try to present the immanent God, the God close at hand, the God who intends to become subjective in each.

For a builder ministry, the preference for worship forms is determined by the results, or the fruitfulness. The builder is looking for new connections and is willing to try new forms.

TOO SUBJECTIVE

As noted, churches with centuries-long heritages have developed church cultures that resist planned expressions of subjective personal experiences. The heritage highlights three cautions about going too far into the subjective.

1. Resistance to individualism. In the tradition, the flock takes precedence over the individual in church life. Privatized experiences are too susceptible to sinfulness. The corrective of the whole community of faith is necessary.
2. Resistance to emotionalism. The descendants of northern European Protestants are still noted for the reserve with which they express emotions. Public displays of strong feelings just plain make many uncomfortable. A more substantive caution is that excessive emotionalism may lead to preferring feelings over careful thought. Inner experiences are not dependable, since they come

and go and differ in strength and intensity. A careful balance between subjective and objective truth is important to maintain in a congregation, and it is easier when the subjective is not emphasized. There is usually no public time or place, for instance, for personal testimonies of changed lives.

3. Preserving the focus on justification by grace alone. Classical Calvinists as well as Lutherans share this focus. Both are doctrinally opposed to views that dilute the treasure of God's gift freely given by stressing the human acts necessary to obtain it. In Reformed circles, this emphasis on human activity is called Arminianism, named after a sixteenth-century Dutch theologian. In practice, especially in revival crusades, it stresses ways to arouse individuals to step forward and profess a conversion experience. Such a personal commitment is exciting. As noted earlier, sharing it can ease entry into a church community. The caution comes from the concerns of pastoral care. What happens when the individual no longer feels as excited and committed as at the time of the professed conversion? Is he or she still saved? Churches with long histories of clear focus on objective truths avoid putting people into that situation.

All three of these cautions are understandable concerns, especially for long-established, infant-baptizing church bodies. The promotion of subjective experiences is risky. By personality, many ministers are risk averse.

OBJECTIVE TRUTH THAT COMPELS

Ministering according to the builder model is inclined to push out the conventional limits on subjectivity in church life. Such experiences become important additional points of connection with Christ and others. And the importance of connecting others to Christ provides the basic motivation for moving into builder ministry. The relationship with Christ has eternal consequences.

Ministry in the builder model is hard work. Why bother? Why try ministries that are beyond the norm in shepherd-oriented church bodies? Why run the risk of conflict by advocating a builder mentality in a congregation accustomed to being shepherded?

The only answer that provides staying power for ministry is the compelling need to reach out with the life-changing Good News of salvation in Christ.

Two kinds of churches will be uncomfortable with the builder emphasis on reaching beyond the congregation. One is the large number of mostly mainline church bodies where objective truth itself has gotten fuzzy, mostly by assumptions about Scripture that weaken its authority for teaching and setting priorities. When the message of eternal salvation only in Christ becomes questionable, the motivation to share it is considerably reduced.

The other kind of churches that will be uncomfortable with a builder ministry is those that stay focused on themselves even though they rejoice in the objective truths of the redeeming Savior. Without a compelling sense of mission, they are usually not ready to consider changes that would make them more accessible to people with backgrounds different from theirs. Builder ministry is hard work. Getting it started can be even harder.

THE CHALLENGE AHEAD

The challenge basic to this book is to help ministers in conservative Protestant infant-baptizing congregations become better builders—and to do this without compromising their theological heritage. So many models of "successful" ministry are clustered under the general term "Evangelical." Many of their practices do not fit churches with infant-baptizing assumptions. But some do. The effort here will be to sort through options for emphasizing personal spiritual experiences in church life.

Because of their heritage, older church bodies are reluctant to talk about "successful" ministry. Yet fruitfulness remains a biblical mandate for ministry. The builder model of ministry, patterned after the apostles Paul and Peter, is ever attuned to results—the fruit. It can certainly remain faithful at the same time.

QUESTIONS FOR DISCUSSION

1. How much do you expect the Holy Spirit's involvement in your church life?
2. Can subjective truth be too subjective?
3. Can objective truth be too objective?
4. How are emotions handled in your church experience?
5. Can infant-baptizing churches focus attention on personal spiritual experiences without compromising their theological heritage?

3

Shepherd: A Great Ministry in the Right Circumstances

This village church is located about a hundred miles south of Chicago near the Indiana border. In its cemetery are the graves of Ernst August Luecke and Wilhelm August Luecke. The first is my grandfather; the second, my great-grandfather. Many of the other headstones are of relatives to one degree or another. The village is Woodworth, Illinois.

The church is St. Paul Evangelical Lutheran. Services began in 1872 in the home of my great-grandfather. He had bought property and moved there in 1872 from Crete, Illinois.

Eight miles from Woodworth is a small church surrounded by cornfields. Ash Grove Lutheran is my mother's church, and its cemetery has the graves of many of my relatives. Five miles from there is St. John Lutheran in the village of Buckley. Ditto its cemetery. This section of Iroquois County between Watseka and Buckley was heavily settled by German immigrants in the 1870s, attracted by rich farmland newly made arable when swampy conditions were drained.

RURAL CHURCHES

This pocket of German Lutherans has counterparts throughout the states of Illinois, Indiana, Iowa, Minnesota, Missouri, Nebraska, Ohio, and Wisconsin. They were populated during the great wave of immigrants from Germany seeking a new start in the 1870s and 1880s. They became the rural base that shaped The Lutheran Church—Missouri Synod. Similar pockets of immigrants from the Lutheran lands of Norway, Sweden, Denmark, and Finland emerged especially in Wisconsin and Minnesota and shaped the Scandinavian synods that eventually all merged into what is now the Evangelical Lutheran Church of America.

The three village churches of my relatives are still alive and well. St. Paul has a membership of 500 with average attendance of 220 and maintains an elementary school. St. John has a membership of 1,000 with average attendance of 380. Those are large churches by Lutheran standards. Ash Grove remains a small church of basically six families.

Pastors in these churches have come and gone, some for short stays, others for longer. To hear my relatives describe pastors, those who were especially valued took good care of the sick and dying. One earned disfavor when he did not come on the day of an elderly relative's death, having been there a week before.

These are shepherd churches. Member families have high loyalty. Together they will survive just about anything a pastor does or does not do, including in one case a very public sex scandal. For pastors who understand the culture and are willing to invest time in relationships, ministry there can be very rewarding.

Significantly, several churches in this area recently asked to become part of the Central Illinois District, which is primarily rural and small town. They had been part of the Northern Illinois District, where suburban Chicago churches set much of the agenda. Rural and suburban congregations increasingly have two different views of what it takes to be church today. Those different needs and perspectives are the matter at hand.

URBAN CHURCHES

In 1932 my father, Rev. Edgar M. Luecke, came to St. Matthew Lutheran Church just several blocks west of the steel mills of the industrial valley in Cleveland, Ohio. St. Matthew's history began in 1884 when German immigrants were pouring into the city for the readily available work. Between 1870 and 1900, national steel production rose about 150-fold, from 77,000 tons to 11,200,000 tons annually. St. Matthew was the daughter church of Immanuel five blocks further north, founded in 1880, which was the daughter church of Trinity, founded in 1853, which was fourteen blocks further north and was the daughter church of Zion on the east side, the first Lutheran presence in 1843.

The story is told of how the first Immanuel pastor would team up with the priest from St. Michael's Catholic Church to work a new street of immigrants. Each took one side and determined whether the German family was Catholic or Lutheran and then gave to the other the names that did not belong to him. They were shepherds gathering their flock. Each of those Lutheran churches was built with a school, gym and bowling alley to better function as a community center for members who wanted to maintained their German language and culture. In the first part of the twentieth century, these were very large and healthy congregations with little difficulty attracting new members who fit in with the old.

This church growth phenomenon was replicated in other urban immigrant centers like Baltimore, Cincinnati, Chicago, Detroit, Milwaukee, Pittsburgh, and St. Louis. Shepherd ministry was demanding because of the large numbers, but nevertheless usually effective. Lutheran identity, ministry and issues were amazingly homogenous across states and regions of the country.

Between 1880 and the Great Depression in both rural and urban settings, the number of congregations in The Lutheran Church—Missouri Synod grew fourfold, from 1,000 to 4,000. That story was similar in other Lutheran synods.

I enjoyed growing up in the vibrant Lutheran community of Cleveland, attending Lutheran elementary and high schools and interacting with youth of other Lutheran congregations. Subordinating oneself to a big community with a long tradition was very rewarding. We knew who we were. Being Lutheran was very important. Being a minister was high achievement in that English-speaking but still ethnically rooted community.

But then after World War II came the next great migration, from city to suburbs. I grew up in a church that every year had smaller attendance and smaller everything. My father did work the neighborhood intensively and had some breakthroughs in a public housing area, but the decline was hard to stop. St. Matthew closed its doors in 1977. The building is now occupied by a Hispanic Pentecostal congregation. The story of closed or almost-dead center-city Lutheran congregations is very familiar in major urban centers.

SUBURBAN CHURCHES

In 1990 I accepted a call to plant a new church in second- and third-ring suburbs south of Cleveland. The arrangement was the same used for decades after the Second World War in suburban church planting. The district bought property and I was a mission developer whose job was to gather a flock. But I knew enough about church growth to realize that looking for Lutherans to attend a Lutheran service would be quite limiting. So we started with a handful of people, meager music resources and a contemporary service. An unanticipated reality was that a community church, Southern Baptist by background, had started nearby several years earlier and was doing what I was attempting, only much better.

From Community of Hope I moved over to the neighboring large congregation, Royal Redeemer Lutheran, as administrative pastor, where I now serve as missions pastor. My successor at Community of Hope has done well in using the contemporary format to build it up to an average attendance of about 220. It is in the process of planting a new church in an older part of Cleveland.

Royal Redeemer, the larger church, was a typical suburban church plant of 1957. Lutherans who had moved to that community were gathered by a vicar. The church did well. In 1968 it built the second and present sanctuary. Under the first two pastors it was important to be Lutheran, especially in liturgical aspects of worship. The present senior pastor came in 1982. In 1990, Royal Redeemer went through wrenching conflict in starting a contemporary service. Sunday morning and Saturday evening contemporary services became the engine of growth, facilitated by the building of a large activity center in 1996. Between 1994 and 2000 average attendance went from 550 to 1,000. We have stayed at that level since.

Those years of growth were exciting times of identifying and putting into place staff, programs and facilities for a builder ministry. The participants now come from a variety of backgrounds other than Lutheran.

Church observers note how frequently a barrier to continued growth exists at the level of 1,000 in attendance, just as there are barriers that add difficulty to growing beyond 200 and then also beyond 500. To grow beyond 1,000 calls for an infrastructure of small groups and group activities that build relationships among participants beyond worship services. New members who have not formed a relationship with someone else in the church in several months tend to become inactive. This process of building secondary connections is hard, endless work. Congregation-wide programs to develop group life look good on paper but often translate poorly into the reality of busy lives. It takes considerable staff time to initiate new groupings. Some are lasting; many are not.

Observations about builder ministry in later chapters will draw on these first-hand experiences of ministry. They will be supplemented by ongoing conversations with colleagues in like-minded churches as well as with the published writings of church leaders trying to do effective ministry today.

CHANGING CIRCUMSTANCES

This excursion through generations serves to highlight three different circumstances or community settings for Lutheran ministry. First, the rural context has a high overlap between the congregation's fellowship and the community within the geographic community, called the parish. Historically, Lutheran churches are parish churches, and ministry is parish ministry. *Parish* is basically a geographic term. Church people in the parish know each other from everyday community life. Often family and relatives abound. People are concerned about what their neighbors think of them. Lutherans tend to thrive there.

The second setting is urban center cities, where, too, for decades congregation members knew each other from shared neighborhood contacts beyond church. That was especially true while large cities had communities of descendants of Northern European immigrants. But the generations after the Second World War made the great migration to the suburbs. The congregations that remained behind demonstrated little ability to rebuild church fellowships with the new people now in that geographic parish. Some were able to continue their lives with members who drove back into the city. But those years and generations are ending. Empty church buildings are reminders that for all its strengths, Lutheran church culture is weak in ability to attract people who were not raised in it. This is true in general of infant-baptizing church bodies, including Presbyterian and Episcopalian.

The third community setting is suburban. This is where most of the country's population growth is happening. Here is almost no overlap between church fellowship, social community and geographic community. Those who show up in a congregation typically know few people from prior relationships. But at least the people who visit seem outwardly similar to those already present. Thus a need to change ways to better build church fellowship may not be readily apparent. Changing to accommodate new people who do not know the church culture does not come easily for most Lutheran churches.

FEWER CHILDREN

The first chapter on issues highlighted the differences between infant baptizing church bodies that retained their European heritage and newer American-based bodies that practice adult believer baptism. The latter, grouped as Evangelicals, have been doing better numerically in recent decades.

The following statistics do not bode well for church bodies that have fashioned their church fellowship practices and culture around raising up children to become the members of the future.

Child Baptisms							
Lutherans				Presbyterians		Episcopalians	
LCMS		ELCA		PCUSA		Episcopalian	
1987	55,758	1987	87,443	1983	50,785	1986	49,039
1997	46,984	1997	82,100	1996	39,060	1996	39,060
2007	27,913	2006	66,166	2006	30,493	2006	30,493

In all cases the number of child baptisms has decreased sharply in the last 20 years. In the LCMS it was 50 percent. The ELCA was 25 percent, but the reference figure 20 years earlier is difficult to compile because the merger was in 1988. The Presbyterians and Episcopalians each declined about 40 percent. No one predicts that those numbers will turn around in the near future. They are a reflection of past decline and now a predictor of continuing decline.

These churches follow the pattern of Belong, Believe, Experience rather than the Experience, Believe, Belong sequence typical for Evangelical churches. Their increasing challenge will be to fold adults from a variety of backgrounds into their fellowships. The builder model of the next chapter works with the assumption that the best way to do that is to become better adept at offering accessible spiritual experiences.

Two trends affected the decline in child baptisms. One is an overall decline in birthrate in the United States. From a peak rate of 25.3 births per 1,000 people in 1958—the middle of the Baby Boom—the birthrate declined to 15.4 twenty years ago and was 13.9 in 2002.[1] There are indeed fewer children, especially in the kinds of neighborhoods where the constituency of mainline churches live.

The other trend was for young adults to leave the congregation or the church body into which they were baptized. The Pew Forum on Religion and Public Life reports a 2007 survey result that 44 percent of Americans left the religious traditions in which they grew up.[2] Child baptisms are down because the young parents who would bring the children are missing. That they are missing can be readily observed in visiting the average mainline congregation. This trend started when Baby Boomers no longer were content to take up their parents' church life. Many dropped out of Christianity altogether. Perhaps more disturbing to churches with long traditions was that many found their way to Evangelical congregations that apparently better met their needs. They did not reject the faith; they rejected their parents' version of church life.

Congregations that are missing parents of young children are now up against another hard fact of ministry today. Young families that are seeking spiritual nourishment understandably prefer congregations with established, attractive children's ministries. These tend to be in larger congregations that have more resources. It is very hard for small churches to turn around their decline through children's ministries.

But there is at least one favorable demographic trend. Life expectancy is increasing. Seniors live longer, and they tend to have more disposable income. Therefore congregations can live longer even without the children.

How long they can continue is an open question. But the day does eventually come when they no longer can afford to pay their shepherd pastor, especially as health costs increase. That is the crisis point beyond which few survive. Then the placement opportunities for shepherd-minded pastors will shrink. Then more ministers may become more open to the changes in outlook that go with builder ministry.

THE DECLINE IN "JOINERS"

There is another more subtle change going on that has hardened the circumstances for church ministry today.

In his 2000 publication *Bowling Alone*, sociologist Robert D. Putnam identified the larger social forces at work in America that also have had great impact on religious organizations.[3] He illustrates it with the striking observation that although the number of bowlers continues to increase, the number of bowling teams and leagues has decreased sharply. Drawing on a large database, Putnam describes how Americans have become increasingly disconnected from one another and how social structures of all sorts have disintegrated.

Putnam demonstrates, for instance, in recent decades an overall decline in sports participation, especially in softball, baseball, volleyball, and football. This is distinct from spectator sports.[4] The declines are sharpest among younger Americans. He observes that among major sports, only bowling comes close to holding its own. Now more Americans are bowling than ever before. But league bowling in organized teams has plummeted in the last twenty years. The chart Putnam presents in the book shows the rate of league participation for men peaked at 8 percent in the 1960s and for women in the late 1970s at 5.5 percent. Then came steep declines down to 2 percent for both. What happened? Putnam sees bowling alone as a symptom of a general social shift away from joining any sort of voluntary organized social activities, and the shift is most clearly seen among younger Americans.

Charts with steep declines can be seen for social organizations of all sorts, including Masonic and animal lodges like the Elks. The same goes for Parent Teachers Association, which peaked in 1960 and declined by two thirds since then. In 1970 two thirds of all Americans attended at least one club meeting in that year; by 1999 the figure was reversed to only one third. Putnam observes, "Active involvement in face-to-face organizations has plummeted, whether we consider organizational records, survey reports, time diaries, or consumer expenditure." Further, such involvement has dropped "at an astonishing rate."[5]

Christian churches do have higher claims, but at a minimum they remain voluntary organized social activities and are subject to similar social and generational dynamics. In Putnam's survey of religious organizations of all types, church membership increased from the 1930s to about 1960, followed by a plateau and then *membership* takes a long, slow slump of roughly ten percent between the 1960s and the 1990s. Church *involvement* in terms of attendance, however, had a steeper drop off. There was a sharp rise in attendance in the first several decades after World War II, but that was followed by a decline of roughly one third between the late 1950s and late 1990s. Putnam observes that this "is very much the same pattern that we noted earlier for secular community-based organizations, as well as for political participation."[6]

Within Protestantism the decline is even greater for mainline churches. Putnam observes: "The fraction of all church members who belong to evangelical churches has risen—probably by roughly one-third in the quarter century after 1960—but for Protestants as a whole, the evangelical gains were not enough to offset the mainline losses."[7] These data do not keep track of differences between urban and rural populations. Undoubtedly the losses in urban areas are much greater than the averages reported in those studies.

In retrospect, the 1950s and 60s may well have been an abnormal time in American church history. Those were the softer times when the senior church body leaders of today had their formative experiences of church life. As that senior generation has difficulty keeping up with changing communication technology today, so have many of them been slow to recognize and cope with the newer realities of church life.

George Barna has a great track record for identifying and reporting trends especially among Protestants. He catches the meaning of these data in the metaphor of a frog in a kettle on a stove. As the temperature of the water goes up the frog seems not to notice and does not jump out—until the water gets so hot the frog no longer can jump, because it is dead.[8]

TAKING A CHURCH COMMUNITY FOR GRANTED

What a wonderful blessing it is for a congregation to be a fellowship that is itself a healthy stable community of people who know and support one another and bring loyalty to their participation. Under such circumstances a shepherd ministry can be well received and successfully done for years to come. The context for ministry can be taken for granted. A maintenance ministry of caring for the spiritual needs of the gathered can be appropriate and is often very rewarding.

Such circumstances are most likely to be found in rural areas and small towns. Long-established church bodies have roughly half their congregations in such contexts. I know this to be true of Lutherans because in a 1998 controlled random survey I did for an article on "Trends among Lutheran Preachers," 54 percent self-reported fitting into that category. [9]

The favorable context of church fellowship overlapping social community and geographic community, however, does not mean such churches have few worries. The migration from country to city is accelerating, especially among young adults. A declining population base will most likely yield smaller congregations. Yet under such circumstances, a change in ministry style will probably not produce much different results.

The challenge is in the expanding suburban and urban areas. Withering congregations in the midst of abundant harvest fields should rightfully raise questions about how to do ministry better. Ministry contexts are not as favorable as they used to be. Congregations that can no longer count on young families to raise up new members need to learn to reach out to adults of all ages and fold them into the fellowship. This is building ministry.

WHAT ARE THE OPTIONS?

To challenge traditional ministry understandings and practices is to raise tension levels in a church body. Any change from the known to something more ambiguous is stressful. This is especially true in churches with high concern that their practices remain consistent with their theology.

One option is simply to excuse half the pastors from the discussion. If their ministry circumstances are still favorable, stay with what is working. Shepherding can be a great ministry. But do so with the understanding that ministry in many other congregations has to be done in social contexts that have changed a lot in recent decades, as described in this chapter.

Congregations change slowly. So do functioning organizations in any other area. The field of organizational behavior is now focusing on changing corporate cultures—something very desirable in the hardened business context of rapidly changing technology. A significant change in an organization's culture usually takes at least seven years of focused effort.

Recognize that changing from a Shepherd Model of ministry to a Builder Model involves some very basic changes in a congregation's culture. There are few quick fixes. It takes long-range leadership commitment. That is hard to sustain without a good understanding of the spiritual as well as the organizational dynamics at work.

Planting a new church is a good way to get a new church culture started. But from my twenty years of interest in following church plants, I observe that the track record of long-established, infant-baptizing church bodies is not impressive in this regard, except sometimes in areas of very rapid population growth. Too often a plant is not able to build up a core group big enough to attract those not already highly committed. One interesting development in this field is the move toward using a large mother church to spin off a smaller group to become the basis of the new fellowship—a practice very common a hundred years ago.

For what follows I chose the option of sidestepping the latest discussions of cutting-edge ministries. More effectively reaching Generation X or the Millennials or twenty-somethings is a direct answer to the missing young generation in traditional congregations. But this is difficult. Recognizing how differently they approach life is sobering, but along with that goes the observation that there are many more subcultures than there used to be. The one best way by which they get built up into self-sustaining church fellowships is by no means clear yet.

To clarify, my focus in what follows is on incremental steps of change that can go on within congregations that carry a heritage they want to respect. In particular the builder emphasis will be fitted to churches whose culture has been shaped by infant baptizing.

The shepherd assumptions, pattern and values discussed in this chapter are highlighted below.

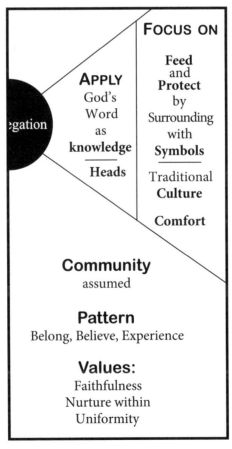

QUESTIONS FOR DISCUSSION

1. In which setting have each of you involved in this discussion had most of your church experience: rural/small town, urban/central city, or suburban?

2. Do you agree or disagree with the observation that Lutheran church culture is weak in ability to attract people who were not raised in it?

3. How do you interpret the statistics showing that infant-baptizing church bodies have reported a significant decline in children baptized in the last twenty years?

4. Do you agree with Robert Putnam's sociological observation that Americans are increasingly disconnected from each other as social structures of all sorts disintegrate?

5. Have you generally assumed that a congregation's continued existence as a fellowship can be taken for granted?

6. In which context would you prefer to minister: rural/small town, urban/central city, growing suburban, mature suburb?

7. What options do you see for a declining church body to turn around and have new growth?

4

Biblical Builder Ministry

Paul of Tarsus was a builder by instinct and mission. He earned his living in the construction trades, as did also Jesus of Nazareth. From sewing or connecting pieces together to make a shelter, Paul moved on easily to connecting people together in church fellowships for the sake of the Gospel.

The distinctive feature of the apostle Paul's ministry is so obvious it might be easily overlooked. His focus was always upon people—not just people in general but particular people in specific places.

Much of the great Christian theological writings over the centuries strove to formulate and refine general principles about God and humans in the propositional statements of doctrine. Their work could easily be written in a special room somewhere, and in fact it usually was: in monasteries in the Middle Ages and in universities since the Reformation. The thinkers were deliberately cut off from lively interaction with everyday people so they could concentrate on their great thoughts.

Paul was no ivory tower theologian. He was a builder who had things to accomplish with and through God's people. His thoughts were focused on practical payoff. His writings are not treatises but letters to people he knew in specific places, like Corinth, Ephesus, Rome, Galatia, Colossae, Philippi, and Thessalonica. They are called occasional letters, written on the occasion of some need that came to his attention. We can wish today that he had been better at what we now call systematic theology. He comes closest to that in his letter to the Romans, but then he ends with greetings to twenty-six specifically named people he knew or had heard about.

RELATIONSHIPS

But Paul does not just think about individual people. He is always looking at them in relationship to others. Fellowship and unity are key concepts. The Greek is *koinonia*, which means sharing something with someone, and is often translated "community." "Fellowship" is closer to the original meaning. Over and over again he writes about fellowship with God and with one another. What do you do with fellowship? You build it up.

Note how Paul continually urges these church people he is addressing to exercise their relationship one to another. Community is not just a symbol. Consider the "one another" passages in his letters:[1]

Love one another	Don't provoke or envy one another
In honor preferring one another	Bear one another's burdens
Don't judge one another	Forbear with one another in love
Receive one another	Forgive one another
Salute one another	Teach and admonish one another
Greet one another	Comfort one another
Serve one another	Edify one another

It is the focus on developing or preserving interactive community that moves Paul beyond a shepherd ministry. Sheep are herd animals. Community can be assumed and the shepherd can afford to spend his time with individual sheep that are ill or have strayed. In Jesus' parable, the shepherd can leave the ninety-nine to look for the one lost because the flock left behind will stay together until he gets back (Matthew 18:10–14; Luke 15:2–7).

In teaching lay pastors in Haiti, I once commented on the presence of goats scattered all over the streets and yards, and I asked them why it is that in the parable of the Last Judgment the sheep get to go to heaven and the goats have to go into eternal fire. Their answer was immediate. Sheep are herd animals; goats are not. Goats wander off on their own. To draw an analogy, Paul was used to dealing with human goats, sinners who want to do things their own way. His leadership challenge was to get them together into community and then to restore that community when they inevitably strayed from the shared Christian life.

TRUTH AS RELATIONSHIP

One of the hard transitions from seminary education into practicing ministry is to put the flesh of real people and their needs on the bones of carefully learned doctrine. It took me years to figure out that ministry is primarily a people business, not a truth-application pursuit. The two have to go together, of course, but real ministry starts with real people. That is where Paul started.

And it is not just about individual persons. Ministry is all about their relationships. Wise, experienced pastors have known this over the centuries. The meaning of this theoretical concept, however, probably only becomes real with experience. A church executive once expressed to me his hope that if he could just communicate one thing to seminary graduates, it would be that relationships are central to ministry. He spent a lot of time cleaning up messes left by new pastors who just could not quite get the hang of this perspective. He acknowledged he himself took years to realize this.

It is easy to think that God's truth is the doctrine or the general principles Paul worked so carefully to enunciate. All we need to do is recognize and believe them, thus making that objective truth subjective. But for Paul there is much more.

For Paul, truth in action is relationships. The faith that counts is the act of trusting in someone, not just agreeing to statements of faith. The Word of God is not just the word from God; it is God in the person of Jesus Christ. Thus Paul emphasizes that we are called into a growing relationship with Christ. He used phrases like "belonging to Christ," "called into fellowship with Christ," "Christ in you," "Christ dwelling in your heart" (Romans 7:4, 1 Corinthians 1:9, Ephesians 3:17, Galatians 2:20). Martin Luther's phrase was "Christ for me." The Good News Bible translates Paul's teaching on reconciliation with God as being made friends with God. God's truth is not completed until there is a response. Thus Jesus did not stop with proclaiming the wonderful truth that "God so loved the world that he sent his Son." The completion is "that whoever believes in him may have eternal life." The two-way relationship is essential.

The relationship between believers is also essential. That's what it means to be in the body of Christ. To be in fellowship with Christ is to be in fellowship with other believers who are part of the same body. In Paul's thought, you can't have one without the other. In Paul's use, fellowship has the meaning of sharing something profound with someone, not just cookies and coffee in the fellowship hour. It is sharing the basics of the new life in Christ that comes with truth as encounter.

One of the hardest parts of trying to build community in congregations today is that participants are usually willing to receive what others offer but often seem reluctant to return time and effort when that part of sharing becomes personally inconvenient. The kind of fellowship Paul is talking about comes from the spiritually new life in Christ that changes priorities even for every-week life.

Having a "personal relationship with Christ" is a phrase one hears frequently among believer-baptizing Evangelicals. The phrase seems somewhat foreign to believers in infant-baptizing churches with European state church backgrounds. That is because over time, truth as encounter gets replaced by truth as doctrine and church as institution. Along the way, the fellowship of church life can become shallow, and church conversation settles in to the small talk so typical of social community. Energy for dynamic church life is then hard to generate.

MOVEMENT

Churches with state church backgrounds have inherited a vocabulary and organizational style that are essentially static. Ministry is basically teaching children to become confirmed and then caring for and protecting them as adults over the years. The truth that gets talked about is in terms of doctrine based on confessional statements pitched to a prince or a deliberative body where determination of the true church will be made. Truth as encounter is not necessary for sustaining church life.

The problem for such historic church bodies is that the "competition" of Evangelical and community churches does have vocabulary and practices that express and promote truth as encounter. They strive to become effective churches, and their emphasis is on truths which are oriented that way. As noted in the first chapter, "effective church" is not in the vocabulary of confessional churches that focus on being the true church.

"Spiritual journey" is typically not in their vocabulary either. The readiness to talk about continual change in one's spiritual life as well as in church life can add expectation and excitement that do not come naturally to churches with static assumptions.

But the topic at hand is Paul and his theological understandings that led him into builder rather than shepherd ministry. He assumes there will be movement toward improvement in personal relationship with Christ and also in the relationships of church as a fellowship.

First, consider individual movement or journey. "Transformation" is his word of choice. He urged the Romans to be transformed by the renewal of their minds (Romans 12:2). For him, transformation is not a one-time event but a continual process of renewal. To the Corinthians he explained that we are being transformed into the Lord's likeness with the ever-increasing glory that comes from the Spirit (2 Corinthians 3:18). "With ever-increasing glory" is the key phrase. The glory is the ministry of the Spirit working within us individually. It keeps getting better, or it can get better with Spirit-oriented ministry. With the Ephesians (3:19) he prayed that the Lord would strengthen them through his Spirit in their inner being so that Christ may dwell in their hearts. The next phrase in the passage is the movement: "that you may be filled to the measure of all the fullness of God" (Ephesians 3:19). In this life no one will ever reach the fullness of Christ. But we can come closer. That's the journey.

In Lutheran heritage, these kinds of transformation can rightfully be considered as "awakenings" to a new higher understanding of and commitment to following Christ.

Now consider the ongoing journey of a congregation. The first fourteen verses of Ephesians 4 present Paul's ministry understanding and approach most fully and concisely. Much more on that in a bit. But for now, note that in 4:13 he applies the same phrase, "the measure of the fullness of Christ," to the body of Christ in Ephesus. It is to be built up until all in fellowship together become completed, attaining the whole measure of the fullness of Christ. The TEV translation is "reaching to the very heights of Christ's full stature." Will any congregation ever become so complete? Not in this life. The objective of builder ministry is to keep moving in that direction. Maintaining a static condition does not do justice to the potential fullness of Christ's body in that place.

In the simple words of a highly respected nineteenth-century church leader,[2] congregations should be asking themselves whether they are going forward or backward, and if backward, they need to repent and do better.

IMPROVING THE GARDEN AND BUILDING

How do we know that the apostle Paul thought of himself as a builder? Because he said so. The third chapter of his first letter to the Corinthians is potent for our present purposes of understanding how he approached his ministry.

In 3:10 Paul describes himself as a master builder. As such, he laid a foundation in Corinth that someone else is now building on. In the Greek version his claim is as "architect."

As such, how did he envision the Christians to whom he was writing? In the verse just before, he describes the material he is working with: "You are God's field, God's building."

This is a distinction between an organic field and an inorganic building that squares with the best of modern thinking about people in organizations. Now we call it organic and mechanistic views and approaches. For years I taught the course The Social Psychology of Work Organizations at the School of Business of Washington University in St. Louis. I gave the M.B.A. students the final exam question on the first day of classes: How would you approach each of the main topics of the course from the viewpoint of mechanistic and then of organic management practices? Mechanistic puts people into boxes and assigns predetermined tasks and relationships. Organic anticipates people adapting to ever-changing tasks and relationships. For punching out aluminum cans by the millions, mechanistic is by far more appropriate. For cutting-edge high-tech design and production, organic will get you more surely where you want to go. You choose one or the other depending on what you are trying to accomplish.

A CONGREGATION AS A GARDEN

Paul's garden/building statement is a transition. In the early part of that chapter he is trying to get this congregation to overcome the growing division between those who want to follow Apollos, an eloquent co-worker of Paul, and those who prefer Paul. He explains that the two men have different tasks. Paul planted the seed, Apollos watered it; but both pursue the same goal. And then comes the absolutely necessary recognition that it is God who grants the growth. Let no minister today claim that he "grew a church" from some number to a bigger one. God did it; he just helped.

What did Paul see when he envisioned these believers as a field? I doubt he was thinking of a farmer's field with a uniform crop in neat rows. In a different letter he envisioned the Ephesians as a body with many different parts. I think Paul here had in mind a garden with many different plants arrayed in a pleasing and complementary manner—some as fruit trees, others as flowers, yet others as shrubs defining borders.

What is the movement that should happen in a garden? The plants at appropriate times should bear the fruit they were created to bear—some as olives or grapes, others as blooming flowers, yet others as colorful leaves. They need to be planted and consistently watered and cultivated for this to happen.

Certainly it is appropriate to ask of a pastor today what are the fruits of his ministry. Something better spiritually should have happened in the shared lives of people of that congregation. Did the garden get better? Or did the plants wither for lack of water or become overgrown with weeds? Were new plants added?

In the 1980s the Church Growth movement captured the attention of many congregational leaders. It served powerfully to focus attention on leadership outcomes. But there were two weaknesses. One is the shorthand that implied growth comes from human leaders rather than from God. The other is the implication that the only growth that counts is the numeric addition of new members. Such an inference was facilitated by the limits of the English language. The German part of the movement stated the outcome much better: *Gemeinde Aufbau*—congregation upbuilding. The German suggests building up individuals and their relationships. Some kind of growth should be going on in and between members as well as in attraction of new members. There should be some improvement to which to point.

How does the organic theme of a garden fit together with the more mechanistic theme of an architect who plans a physical structure? Architects, like all other modern builders, have gotten specialized. Some present themselves now as landscape architects who design plantings, walkways and interesting clusters for the space outside the physical building. That is a wonderful analogy for how a pastoral leader should think of himself—as a landscape architect of congregational life.

A CONGREGATION AS A BUILDING

Now let's follow the transition to the building part of how Paul envisioned the Corinthians. In his first letter, 3:10–14, he says, you are God's building, and as an architect I laid a foundation. Those who build on it should be careful. Your ministry can be discerned according to its quality; it can be done with gold or straw or gradations in between. That is, the outcome can be precious and lasting, or makeshift and passing. The quality of each man's work will be tested.

The word he used for this building comes from his favorite vocabulary for describing his work. In the Greek it is *oikodome*. The verb is *oikodomein*. The word has two parts: *oikos*, meaning house, and *domein*, meaning to build. *Oikos* in the Greek has many meanings, befitting its heavy usage. It can be a physical structure but also the people who live in that house, the household. *Oikos* is the only Greek word available for what we call a family today. More than blood relatives, it is all those whose lives revolve around the villa—slaves as well as friends. *Oikos* is the word Paul used for what we now call house churches—Christians gathered in the household of specifically named people. In this sense it is really a fellowship. In all, Paul uses noun and verb variations of *oikodome/oikodomein* 32 times in his writings.[3]

I think it legitimate at points to translate Paul's use of *oikodomein* as to "build up fellowship." That translation opens up new meaning for many familiar passages, starting with the one in 1 Corinthians 3 that we just looked at. Paul laid the foundation but someone else is building fellowship on it; do be careful how you build up fellowship. "Edification" is a familiar translation that is usually given a special religious flavor. It is simply the Latin version of this Greek word—to make a structure (edifice). Thus Paul warns the Corinthians that everything may be permissible, but not everything builds up fellowship (edifies). When they gather, the chosen songs and words must be done to build up fellowship (for edification). They should make every effort to do what leads to peace and to being built together as a fellowship. Everything Paul does is for building up their fellowship. (See 1 Corinthians 10:23, 14:26, 14:19; 2 Corinthians 12:19.)

The term "building up" inherently carries with it the notion of movement. Something is changing. If a congregation as a garden is to bear appropriate fruit, what should be the outcome of that congregation as a building? The end of the building passage in chapter 3 reminds the Ephesians they are to be built up into a temple in which the Holy Spirit lives. The result of good leadership should be some improvement in the temple of those people at that place.

A reasonable question to any congregation and its pastor is, How is your temple doing? Is it being built up or falling down? Where is the activity of building up most evident? What is the construction team of leaders working on now?

PREPARE FELLOW MEMBERS FOR MINISTRIES THAT BUILD UP THE BODY OF CHRIST

Let's move now to the most significant summary passage of what church ministry for Paul is all about. It is in the fourth chapter of his letter to the Ephesians. According to the NIV, "It was he [Christ] who gave some to be apostles, some to be prophets, some to be evangelists and some to be pastors and teachers to prepare God's people for works of service, so that the body of Christ may be built up until we all reach unity in the faith and in the knowledge of the of the Son of God and become mature, attaining to the whole measure of the fullness of Christ" (4:11–13).

The Greek text for these lines deserves serious attention. (1) Should there be a comma between the phrase "prepare God's people" and "for works of service? (2) Is "service" the best translation for the Greek in the text? (3) How best should the key Greek word translated "prepare" be understood?

First, does "works of service" modify "preparing God's people," or is it a second function of the leaders. Thus, is it the called ministers doing the preparing *and* the works of service, or are these actions something all God's people do? The latter reading highlights ministry done by the laity. As scholar John Jefferson Davis shows, most translation of the past sixty years (NIV, New English Bible, Today's English Version [Good News], New King James, and New Revised Standard) go with the broader understanding.[4]

Second, the Greek word for service in "works of service" gives us "deacon," which basically means helper. The Latin version of *deaconia* is *ministerium*. The English "minister" in church usage is ambiguous. Some would have it refer only to the ordained leaders. But Paul is saying that everyone in that congregation is a minister, a deacon, a helper with important work to do. The leaders' job is to get them ready so they can do the wide range of ministries or services that build up the body.

The key Greek word for getting them ready is *katartismos*, in noun form to describe action but consistently translated as a verb. According to *The Theological Dictionary of the New Testament*,[5] this word group's verb form *katartizo* can have the sense of "to equip," but also the sense of "to regulate," which conveys a standard to which something is adjusted. According to the *Greek-English Lexicon of the New Testament*,[6] the broader Hellenic culture sometimes used it as a medical term for setting a bone. The King James translation as "to perfect," that is, to conform to an ideal standard, carries this sense of putting in order. 1 Corinthians 1:10 uses the *katartizo* verb to urge that the Corinthians be perfectly united (fitted together). In Hebrews 11:3, at God's command the universe was formed (fitted together). Regulation involves restoration to the right standard. In 1 Peter 5:11 Peter uses the *kartartizo* verb to describe how, "after you have suffered a little while, (God) will restore you and make you strong, firm and steadfast." It is also the meaning in Galatians 6:1—"restore him [the one caught in sin] gently."

Align is an English word that carries such meaning, that is, getting into correct relative position. The interpretation of *kartartizmos* as "regulate" or "align" seems justified. Thus Paul is urging these leaders to get fellow members aligned for their ministries—aligned with Gospel teaching as well as relationally aligned with each other.

The sense of "to align" fits well with Paul's builder theme—get the walls aligned, that is, perpendicular, straight and lined up with each other. This pastoral work begins with spiritual preparation of each member, especially through recognition of how the Spirit has gifted them for the good of the congregation—Paul's teaching in the 12th chapter of his letter to the Corinthians—and aims at getting them organized to put their giftedness to work for building up their common fellowship. The apostle Peter makes this organizational understanding explicit in 1 Peter 4:10: "Each one should use whatever gift he has received to serve others, faithfully administering God's grace in its various forms."

Moving on, the central phrase in the long and complicated sentence (Ephesians 4:11–13) is "so that the body of Christ may be built up." The leaders begin by teaching and organizing members of that congregation in Ephesus, unleashing them for their work, and then they continue leading them until their particular body of Christ has been built up to the very heights of the fullness of Christ.

At first glance, "building the body" may seem a mixed metaphor, when associating building with organic bodies. Here is how Paul works the two together a few verses later in chapter 4: "Instead, speaking the truth in love, we will in all things grow up into him who is the Head, that is, Christ. From him the whole body, joined and held together by every supporting ligament, grows and builds itself up in love, as each part does its work."

To the Corinthians, Paul identifies himself as an architect, or the master builder. Earlier in chapter 2 he gives an architect's rendering of how the project fits together: "Consequently, you are no longer foreigners and aliens, but fellow citizens with God's people and members of God's household, built on the foundation of the apostles and prophets, with Christ Jesus himself as the chief cornerstone. In him the whole building is joined together and rises to become a holy temple in the Lord. And in him you too are being built together to become a dwelling in which God lives by his Spirit."

MULTIPLYING RELATIONSHIPS

In his day-to-day ministry (in Ephesus and Corinth, for instance), in addition to his teaching of the Gospel, Paul emphasized and modeled relationships within the congregation. The same can be said for wise shepherd ministers. But there is a big difference in how these two approaches to ministry go about developing relationships among those in a congregation.

As described in the workweek of Pastor Schaefer in chapter 1, the shepherd does it through one-by-one relationships between himself and others. He carefully develops relationships with individual members and is there to support each one in need by teaching, guidance, and care. This is the "pastoral relationship." It can be profoundly satisfying to both pastor and parishioner.

As described in the week of Pastor Baumann, the builder gets other leaders involved in developing relationships between members. These can be Bible study or small group leaders as well as leaders of many different ministry teams. These relationships can be at a level much deeper than found in typical committees.

The pattern of relationships with a shepherd minister looks like a wheel with spokes all going to the one hub of the minister.

A pastor as hub can handle a limited number of spokes, perhaps 150 to 200. Beyond that, he gets overextended and often burns out. The demands are too many. The congregation usually does not expand.

The pattern with builder ministers has lots of little wheels with spokes to members.

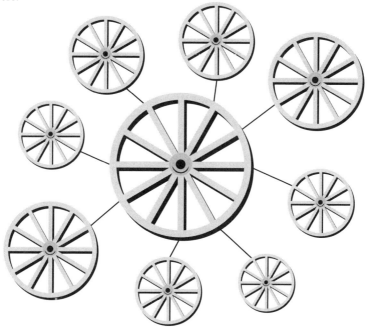

The pastor's efforts go into relationships with the hub leaders of these little wheels. Expansion potential is practically unlimited for leaders with organizational abilities. The members serving as smaller hubs can take on leadership roles for evangelism and outreach, assimilation, small groups, discipleship, spiritual gift administration, adult education, stewardship, mission teams, or church planting.

Remember from the discussion of Ephesians 4 that the job of apostles, prophets, evangelists, pastors and teachers is to get fellow ministers aligned for building up the body of Christ in that place. Paul's insight turns the traditional ministry relationship 180 degrees. Instead of the ordained ministering to members as recipients, the members are the ministers and the ordained prepares leaders to support the members in their various ministries and relationships.

But this concept cannot be well appreciated without understanding Paul's teaching on spiritual gifts administration. That comes in the next chapter.

How do we know that Paul did not pursue shepherd ministry? Because most of the time he was gone from any of the churches he planted, either on a mission trip or in prison. He had to depend on others. Of those he greets at the end of his letter to the Romans, at least three and probably eight were identified as heads of house churches.

CARPENTER, CONTRACTOR, ARCHITECT

Paul's self-description as architect opens up perspectives on other kinds of builders. The second part of the Greek "architect" gives us the English word *technician*. The architect is the "master technician." In today's usage, a technician more narrowly refers to somebody who does the hands-on work, whether laying bricks or fixing refrigerators. We can use a carpenter as the representative of all hands-on builders. In their construction trades, Jesus and Paul were technicians, Jesus with hammer and Paul with needles.

In construction work today, the architect no longer does hands-on building beyond drawing the plans. Also, there is usually a third type of builder between the architect with the overall plan and the carpenters, plumbers, electricians, etc., who do the hands-on work. This is the contractor, who finds the workers and material and then brings them together at the right time. In addition to being an architect, Paul did his ministry as a contractor. For the Corinthians in chapter 12, he lists the different kinds of ministries present among members. With the similar list in Romans 12, he adds the exhortation for each to put that ministry into action: "If it is serving, let him serve; if it is teaching, let him teach; if it is encouraging, let him encourage, if it is contributing to the needs of others let him give generously; if it is leadership, let him govern diligently; if it is showing mercy, let him do it cheerfully" (NIV). This is contractor talk.

The difference between shepherd and builder ministries can be recognized with reference to these three kinds of builder. The shepherd basically functions as the hands-on minister who does all the preaching, teaching, caregiving and any other form of ministry in the congregation. Call it a carpenter ministry. Congregations find this very satisfying, as do many pastors. The limits have already been recognized.

In the builder paradigm, the members do much of the hands-on ministry and the pastor is the contractor and encourager. Any change in role of the minister in this direction is likely to be resisted by established congregations.

A change toward architectural ministry is often considered unwelcome in shepherd congregations. The basics of purpose, structure, and activities of the congregation are carried forward by tradition. In builder ministry, a congregation as temple of the Spirit can be built up in all sorts of new and different ways. The minister as architect has to cast and sell the vision of what that congregation can become as it tries to reach to the very heights of Christ's fullness in that location.

PETER, TOO, WAS A BUILDER

The apostle Paul was a colleague of the apostle Peter. They had their differences. But they really thought much alike. Here is Peter's version of builder imagery:

> "As you come to him, the Living Stone—rejected by men but chosen by God and precious to him—you also, like living stones, are being built into a

spiritual house to be a priesthood, offering spiritual sacrifices acceptable to God though Jesus Christ" (1 Peter 2:4–5).

The passive verb implies that, ultimately, God is doing the building. Paul would agree with this view. Switching to the plant metaphor, he explained to the Corinthians (1 Corinthians 3:6) that while he planted and Apollos watered, God is the one who gave the growth.

The characteristics of the builder discussed in this chapter are highlighted below.

QUESTIONS FOR DISCUSSION

1. Do you agree with the assertion that for Paul ministry was primarily about relationships?
2. How does truth as relationship differ from truth as doctrine?
3. Are you comfortable talking about your own personal spiritual journey?

4. How important is it in your thinking that a congregation be in movement, that is, going forward or backward?

5. What kind of words do you use to describe a congregation as healthy or unhealthy? As moving forward or going backward?

6. Does the distinction between church as garden or as building open up insights for you?

7. In your thinking, what does a fruitful ministry look like?

8. What kind of images would you use to describe the kind of building a congregation can be?

9. How have you understood the meaning of Ephesians 4:10 according to the usual translation of equipping or preparing the saints for works of service?

10. How comfortable are you with the interpretation of getting church members aligned for ministries that build up the body of Christ?

11. How important is it to you to multiply relationships in a congregation? How would you go about it?

12. Would you prefer carpenter, contractor or architectural ministry?

5

The Fellowship Builder's Toolbox

What are the basic tools for a minister's work—shepherd or builder? They have remained the same since the beginning: God's Word and the Sacraments. At least this can be said for Protestant infant-baptizing church bodies with European state church backgrounds: Lutheran, Presbyterian, and Episcopalian. The Reformed, like Presbyterians, use the term "ordinances" instead of "sacraments."

The discussion of tools in this chapter is organized around differing approaches toward preaching the Word, celebrating the sacraments, planning worship, doing prayer, and pursuing spiritual disciplines. The intent is to identify new or additional ways to build up fellowship in a congregation.

The tools discussed in this chapter are:

The well-communicated Word

The Sacraments

Experiential worship

Shared prayer

Small-group Bible study and prayer

Sacrificial giving

Service projects

Individual confession and absolution

Spiritual guidance

Faith retreats

Short-term mission trips

The topics in this chapter reflect the emphases set out in the third columns from the center of the paradigm chart.

EMPHASIZE	EMPHASIZE
Well-communicated **Word**	Proclaimed **Word**
Sacraments In balance	Reliance on **Sacraments**
Engaging **Worship**	Liturgical **worship**
Shared **Prayer**	Formal and personal **prayer**
Disciplines esp. individual	
Plus: Small groups Renewal weekends Mission trips	**Disciplines** esp. corporate

WORD AND SACRAMENTS

THE WELL-COMMUNICATED WORD

Advances in technology have opened up a host of new possibilities for better communication at reasonable costs that were not available twenty-five years ago.

These begin with sophisticated high fidelity multi-speaker sound systems that are a considerable advancement over the two-speaker public address equipment that began appearing in churches in the middle of the twentieth century. No longer should a listener of any age have to strain to make out the words of a sermon or prayer.

Visuals can be much more readily presented. Powerful video projectors that cost $25,000 fifteen years ago are now available for a tenth that amount. Software programming for PowerPoint visual presentations is now available at little expense on entry-level laptop or desktop computers. Video editing that had to be done ten years ago in a television studio can now be accomplished with inexpensive software using $300 digital camcorders. Talent to do such video development is often available among teenagers. Any congregation with the will to do multimedia communication can readily find the way.

Where you find a sanctuary with video-projecting capabilities and a booth with multichannel mixer boxes, there is probably a builder minister. While not always so, where there is a sanctuary with just 1950s speakers and a few stationary microphones at the lectern, pulpit and altar, there is usually a shepherd minister.

But what is involved in the well-communicated Word goes deeper than good usage of technology, as important as that is.

PROCLAMATION OR COMMUNICATION?

In a provocative and well-written essay,[1] Robert W. Schaibley asserts that preaching should be proclamation, not communication. He resists pronouncements that too much preaching "fails to communicate," and that it does not "establish contact with the hearers." The reason for his view is opposition to an often-stated assumption that preaching needs to deliver what the person in the pew "wants to hear."

If by what they "want to hear" he means human wisdom and implies resistance to foolishness of the Gospel, I agree. But in common usage, communication usually means a concern that the signals sent by the presenter are also received and understood by the hearer. Proclamation too often means preaching the truth in language and cultural terms convenient to the speaker. Good communication accepts the responsibility to translate those truths into the cultural equivalents the hearer knows today. Proclamation too often starts and ends with the specialized language and symbols within easy reach of the speaker. Communication starts with understanding the hearer and stretching to reach his or her language and frame of reference. Instead of using the theological language of justification and reconciliation, a communicator might talk about being made right with God and God making us his friend. The challenge is to be sure the truth stays the same with either approach.

A tip-off to Schaibley's orientation to shepherd ministry is his assertion that preaching should provide "food for the faithful."[2] He assumes the presence of a faithful and loyal congregation committed to hearing and deciphering Biblical truth.

But I think he would be sympathetic with the kind of communication I am trying to describe. He encourages all preachers to play "search and destroy" with their manuscript, deleting every churchly buzzword and replacing it with something more understandable. "See what happens when you can't use the word Gospel, and instead you must just preach Gospel, rather than preach about Gospel. . . . Instead of talking about 'faith,' rework that sermon so that through your proclamation you are preaching faith into your hearer."[3] I would rephrase this to say, Don't just present abstract doctrinal concepts, describe the relationships they stand for.

LECTIONARY OR TOPICAL PREACHING?

Through long tradition, infant-baptizing church bodies develop and use a lectionary of assigned readings for each Sunday of the church year. Using that as the basis for the sermon is called *lectionary preaching*. A common alternative is topical preaching, organizing a sermon around a topic of the preacher's choosing. Topics are often done in series.

In 1998 I had the opportunity to do a carefully chosen random survey of Lutheran pastors (with a 33 percent response rate, totaling 169 completed questionnaires) to discover trends in preaching. Not surprisingly, 86 percent identified *lectionary preaching* as their most characteristic approach. I surveyed a second group (with a 38 percent response rate totaling 19 questionnaires) deliberately biased to represent "trendsetters," pastors known to be doing innovative ministry. In contrast to the 86 percent who do *lectionary* preaching, 67% of the trendsetters identified *topical preaching* as their usual approach. Ninety percent of them grouped themes into a multipart series.[4]

I think they were following the logic of good communication: Start with the questions or concerns a hearer has in his or her own frame of reference and speak God's truth to that. Preaching on "The Church Triumphant" would probably miss. But a series on "Where Is God When You Need Him" or "Big Questions of Faith" is more likely to connect.

Lectionary preaching tends to be deductive: Here is God's Word for today; let's apply it to our lives. Topical preaching in series tends to be inductive: Here is a concern you might have; let's see what God's Word says about it.

Consider whether drawing new people into the fellowship of a congregation is more likely to happen with inductive, topical preaching than with deductive lectionary preaching. In my experience, good topical preaching is more demanding of the preacher than lectionary preaching, for which there are many resources available.

CELEBRATING SACRAMENTS

Anglicans have always focused on the Lord's Supper for their weekly worship. Lutherans have changed their worship culture dramatically in the last century by celebrating the Lord's Supper much more frequently. Before the twentieth century the norm was once every three months; next came a move toward monthly, then to twice a month. According to the same survey of trends, 40 percent of Lutheran congregations now celebrate this sacrament weekly, another 45 percent biweekly and only 15 percent monthly.[5]

Along with this change in frequency has come an almost necessary change in the importance of the sermon. In general, as the liturgy increased, preaching decreased. The norm for sermon length through the early part of the twentieth century was 30 to 45 minutes. Now two out of three Lutheran preachers aim for a sermon of less than 15 minutes. Younger preachers are even more inclined to do short sermons. The claim in preaching classes is that listeners have an attention span of no more than 12 minutes. Try telling that to popular motivational speakers today who regularly do attention-holding presentations for 45 minutes.

Consider how much time in worship is devoted over three months to celebrating the sacrament weekly at 20 minutes for consecration and distribution. That would total 260 minutes over 13 weeks. Preaching 12-minute sermons would add up to 156 minutes of preaching over 13 weeks. Now compare that to the earlier average of 40 minutes of preaching with one quarterly celebration that took half an hour. The 520 minutes of preaching (40 minutes x 13 Sundays) compared to 30 minutes of Lord's Supper over 13 weeks is out of balance in one direction. But might the current average of 260 minutes of communion compared to 156 minutes of sermon be out of balance in the other direction? Old-time Lutherans (a century or longer ago) were ever vigilant against "sacramentalism"—giving the sacraments more attention than the Word. Is there important wisdom in their earlier version of church culture?

Liturgical scholar James White points out that while at Luther's time the mass was celebrated at every service, often it was by the priest alone. Individuals received the sacrament only several times a year.[6] Distribution time was short. Martin Luther's printed sermons are much longer than a twelve-minute homily.

On the other hand, more could be made out of Baptism. It is a once-in-a-lifetime event, usually for an infant who cannot remember it. Lutheran churches learned how to make it twice in a lifetime by regarding teen confirmation as a personal affirmation of Baptism. In my congregation it is an annual remembrance. We invite all baptized worshippers to come forward for a personal re-affirmation of Baptism on the second Sunday of January, when observing the Baptism of Jesus.

EXPERIENTIAL WORSHIP

The rationale for many of the changes in format now characterized as contemporary worship is to improve communication with the participants by reducing barriers to their engagement. Getting out from behind the pulpit and closer to the hearers is a simple change. In addition, having song leaders visible up front with sound amplification makes songs easier to follow and to sing, especially new songs. Having the words projected on a screen enables participants to watch the leaders better and to identify more readily with others in the congregation. Grouping songs together into extended medleys can allow a build-up of emotional engagement. Praise choruses seem to do so better than hymns of previous centuries. An instrumental ensemble with drums can carry the momentum better than an organ. Making shifts from the hymnal order of service permits simplification of the order as well as more informality.

Many talk about "worship wars" going on in church bodies. For infant-baptizing churches this usually pits, in shorthand, liturgical worship against contemporary worship. Such a view is expressed mostly by advocates of renewing ancient liturgies, preferably from the fourth century of the Christian church. This liturgical renewal started getting popular among Protestants just since the 1950s.

From the viewpoint of advocates of contemporary worship, the war is long over. Contemporary worship is well established, especially among growing congregations. In my nine-year-old survey, 43 percent of the larger group of randomly selected ministers were doing some version of contemporary worship in at least one service. By now I am sure that is closer to half. In the same larger group, 88 percent said they also regularly use a complete hymnal service setting in at least one service. Using a variety of worship forms seems by now a well-established practice.

Here is why. Of those who had at least one contemporary worship service, 60 percent self-reported growth in attendance, compared to 38 percent who did only traditional worship. That such variety in itself is important, by the way, came to light with a side calculation. Of the congregations with two or more services, the ones that had the second service different in format from the first—whether or not it was contemporary—57 percent reported growth compared to 28 percent for those who did the same service both times.

Recall the second grouping of ministers selected as trendsetters, mostly on the basis of having a contemporary worship service. More than four out of five of them (83 percent) reported growth in attendance of 10 percent or more in the previous five years. That figure compares to only 24 percent from the random sample reporting similar growth.

The path toward more effectiveness in building up church fellowship seems rather apparent in these data.

Worship scholar James Alan Waddell recently observed rightfully how the war mentality, or the polarization in worship forms, is unhealthy for a church body. In his view, the momentum of the discussion seems in two opposite directions. One side considers anything with the appearance of "contemporary" to be participation in false doctrine. To their frustration, the other side, which makes use of contemporary forms, goes about its business ignoring the discourse altogether.[7] For the other side, war is over. They have gone on to discussions of ministry topics other than worship.

It would be a shame if the gap gets bigger between builder ministry, with its tendency toward contemporary forms, and shepherd ministry, with its tendency to assume specialized liturgical familiarity on the part of those who gather to worship.

Maybe the discussion should be reframed in terms of variety of worship forms rather than sameness.

To reframe the discussion yet another way, does cultivating the ground of a congregation's worship life with a variety of forms tend to engage worshipers—old and new—in ways by which the Holy Spirit can more readily touch hearts? Many are the ministers who report that their largest attendance is in contemporary services, which are also the ones through which most new members come.

PRAYER AND SPIRITUAL DISCIPLINES

SHARED PRAYER

Prayer is the heartbeat of Christian life. It should be for a congregation, too. How many different congregational prayer cultures can there be?

In the shepherd tradition, prayer in church is best left to the shepherd, the minister. He offers prayers in behalf of the congregation as part of the worship service. This is also the time to bring before God all those who are ill or the families of those who have departed. The *pastoral* prayer and any others in a worship service are well prepared or scripted. In many very traditional congregations it is the pastor who beyond Sundays also opens most meetings and events with a prayer.

In this approach personal *individual* prayer should certainly be done, but it is little discussed. It is usually thought of as "closet prayer"—alone and in private, following Jesus' teaching that we should not pray to be seen by men; rather go into your room, close the door and pray to your Father (Matthew 6:5–6). In the shepherd tradition, use of a book of prayers was highly recommended. I have the German prayer book of one of my uncles. It was given to him at his confirmation by the pastor, who also admonished him to use these prayers, otherwise he might say his prayers wrong.

Traditional shepherd churches with pastoral focus on teaching Biblical truth tend to produce members who are hesitant to use their own words in prayer or witness, lest they get it wrong. Asking old-time cradle Lutherans to say a prayer of their own out loud in public is almost as uncomfortable for them as responding to an altar call might be for others. This reluctance is not a strength of inherited church culture.

On the other hand, sharing informal prayers out loud with fellow Christians can be a great opportunity to build up relationships between them. Fostering ministries of prayer comes naturally to the builder mentality, not only for offering more prayers but especially to build up fellowship.

How can prayer in a congregation be organized into shared prayer ministries? Here are some expressions found in many congregations today: prayer chains, cyber prayer (e-mailed distribution of requests), weekly intercessory prayer groups, altar prayer, prayer teams, special prayer services, special prayer campaigns and courses on prayer. None of these are in the old tradition.

In a random survey of Lutheran pastors done in 2002 (with 366 responses and a response rate of 37 percent),[8] I asked about the presence of any of these shared prayer ministries in their congregation. If three of these possibilities were checked, that congregation was considered to have an organized prayer ministry. By that definition, shared organized prayer ministries already then existed in one out of five Lutheran congregations.

Certainly all would agree that this shift in a congregation's prayer culture is positive.

By the way, pastors in those 20 percent of churches with an organized prayer ministry are more likely than others to know someone who has experienced a miracle and to believe that supernatural miraculous healings are possible today.[9] Such experiences provide additional motivation to pray.

SPIRITUAL DISCIPLINES

Spirituality in general is a popular topic in America today. Most of the efforts are simply elevation of the human spirit over material pursuits. A good definition of spirituality that is Christian is offered by British scholar Alister McGrath: "The quest for a fulfilled and authentic Christian existence that brings together the fundamental ideas of Christianity and the whole experience of living out this faith."[10] He highlights how "spirituality" has gained wide acceptance in the recent past as the preferred way of referring to aspects of the devotional practices of a Christian, and especially the interior individual experience of believers.

I prefer to look at spirituality as the ways we cultivate the soil for the Holy Spirit's work in our lives. This includes personal life as well as corporate church life. How do we get ourselves placed where the Spirit can more readily touch our lives?

Disciplines for spiritual life have received new attention among Protestants in the last thirty years. The now-classic presentation is by Richard J. Foster in *Celebration of Discipline: The Path to Spiritual Growth* (1978). Another good accounting from a grace-oriented Protestant perspective is by Dallas Willard, *The Spirit of the Disciplines: Understanding How God Changes Lives* (1988).

Spiritual disciplines have been practiced among Roman Catholic and Orthodox Christians over the centuries. Their practices sometimes appear to slip into the kinds of works-righteousness Reformation Christians protested against. But if used wisely, these disciplines can be helpful for the spiritual growth that comes from the Holy Spirit.

A discipline is an orderly or prescribed pattern of behavior one pursues toward reaching an objective. While in common usage the term has negative connotations of punishment, disciplines can be freely chosen for positive results. Most professionals work within disciplines developed for their work. My shorthand definition is that a discipline is what you do even when you don't feel like it.

Foster presents twelve classic Christian disciplines in three groupings:

Inward Disciplines	Outward Disciplines	Corporate Disciplines
meditation	simplicity	confession
prayer	solitude	worship
fasting	submission	guidance
study	service	celebration

This is not the place to do a teaching on all twelve. Rather, I will comment on which disciplines are already well utilized in shepherd churches and which could be additionally emphasized for builder purposes.

Among the corporate disciplines, weekly attendance at a worship service is the hallmark of a well-functioning shepherd church. That's just what you do. In that service, Lutherans jointly confess their sins to establish their identity as sinners and then receive an absolution to set them up for the rest of the time of praise and hearing God's Word. Celebrations bring joy to life, and the church year as well as fellowship functions regularly bring occasions to celebrate. Of the outward disciplines, Lutherans have excelled at service to meet the needs of others. Witness the extensive network of Lutheran social service agencies in most metropolitan areas of the United States.

In contrast to corporate disciplines, personal disciplines are usually not well developed among Lutherans. While organized Bible study is offered by almost all Lutheran churches, the percentage of their worship attendees who also are in Bible class is notoriously low, compared, for instance, to Baptist culture.

The key to building up lasting and church-changing relationships is to facilitate ways for the Holy Spirit to transform individual lives. This can be done especially through personal inward disciplines. A congregation's leaders can regularly emphasize, model and provide resources for a personal time of Scripture reading, meditation and prayer. They might provide a schedule for daily Bible readings and prayer, and they can make frequent reference to insights or experiences these daily readings stimulated. Some congregations expect such a discipline of all who take on leadership responsibility.

Of the twelve disciplines Foster highlights, simplicity, solitude and fasting have not gotten much traction among Protestants. But fasting involves more than foregoing food for a set period of time. It can include a commitment to do without personal use of a portion of one's income by committing it off the top to God's work. While a tithe literally means 10 percent, the discipline works with any percentage that is faithfully set aside and offered for Kingdom work.

Such tithing has long been a goal in churches. It can be a powerful personal discipline of having one's faith stretched. This commitment also brings greater readiness for other aspects of spiritual growth. It also yields congregations with more resources to do ministry.

SOME FELLOWSHIP BUILDING TOOLS NEW TO PROTESTANTS IN RECENT DECADES

Like promoting spiritual disciplines, working with the tools of organizing and offering small groups, renewal weekends and mission trips can be thought of as designing special experiences for those who will participate. "Designing experiences" would not appear in a conventional listing of ministry tasks, like preaching, teaching, and counseling. But it can be a useful concept for describing tasks that builder ministry can take on.

SMALL-GROUP MINISTRY

The fellowship-building benefits of promoting and sustaining small groups are obvious. Deeper relations can happen in regular meetings with a dozen or so others than when trying to interact with hundreds at a worship service. Small groups in a congregation have, of course, been around in some form since the house churches of Paul. But at times, pastors of shepherd congregations have resisted subgroups meeting together without the pastor's presence. Typically, groups in Protestant congregations now meet for organized shared prayer and Bible study. Earlier efforts to foster small groups just for social fellowship in a congregation did not sustain themselves very well. Better results come when groups have a spiritual task to do, like praying and studying the Bible together.

When in 1990 I came to Cleveland to plant a new congregation, I emphasized small-group evangelism. I aimed it with some success especially at apartment complexes with high turnover of residents. The groups I organized and offered had the appeal of letting new neighbors meet each other.

The builder ministers I know now take for granted the need for small-group ministry. In some communities, small-group ministry is easier to start and maintain than in others. It is harder to do in church cultures that have not pursued small groups in the past, and it is also harder in stable social communities with extended family relationships. In general, promoting and supporting small-group fellowship is an uphill ministry that takes careful, sustained staff attention.

Helpful resources are readily available. Just do a Google search for "small-group ministry."

SPIRITUAL RENEWAL WEEKENDS

The most successful spiritual renewal weekends are highly organized within a long-established structure. Originating among Roman Catholics, these weekends are called *Cursillo*, Spanish for "short course." The event is usually described as a faith journey. In Methodist circles it is called Walk to Emmaus. A well-established Lutheran version is known as Via de Cristo (www.viadecristo.org). They usually run from Thursday evening to Sunday afternoon. This time commitment is a limiting factor. The large Upper Arlington Lutheran Church in Columbus, Ohio, has adapted its own version starting Friday evening.

All these well-established intensive programs feature presentations by individual laypeople on an assigned topic about how they personally have discovered something new in their spiritual life. The topics I am familiar with are the nine fruits of the Spirit in Galatians 5. After each presentation, smaller groupings of the participants discuss application of that topic and presentation to their own lives. In my experience, the well-thought-out sharing by a layperson like themselves can often have greater personal impact than a message from the professional ordained minister.

These events are hard to sustain because they are so labor-intensive for the presenting team. The team of ten or so meet enough times to critique the presentation of each member. Some who have participated in a renewal weekend are asked to join a new team for the next event. The most personal transformation happens among the presenting team. I enjoyed helping one presenter realize that the spiritual changes he celebrated in his life came soon after teaching the two-year Bethel Bible Series.

A local Reformed church I know has done well in building up its membership and attendance through Reconciliation Renewal weekends offered twice a year. These become an opportunity for members to invite non-churched friends to what can be a powerful personal experience.

Spiritual retreats have a long history among Roman Catholics. These help balance out the highly formal liturgical worship in those churches. Unfortunately, when Protestants picked up Catholic-style worship, they did not also bring the personal retreat part of that culture.

SHORT-TERM MISSION TRIPS

The decrease in airfare relative to inflation over the last twenty years has opened up a ministry tool that can have tremendous impact on those who participate. Also helpful is a general increase in personal disposable income over those years. Now a large number of Protestants and Catholics pursue the opportunity of joining a short-term mission team to distant parts of the country and of the world. The common length of such a trip is one week. Some call it a vacation with a purpose.

There is a huge movement among ordinary Christians in wealthy America to go on such missions. It is aided by the appearance of many para-church organizations that specialize in organizing and conducting short-term missions. Someday the secular media will take notice and report on this movement and how these missions are affecting so many lives.

I have participated in and led many such teams that did medical missions, or offered Vacation Bible School, or offered an eyeglass clinic, or helped with construction, or taught English as a second language, or taught lay pastors.

Part of the joy for me, beyond reaching out to others, is to see the reaction of first-time participants. A frequent reflection is that this was a "life changing" experience for them. Some of that has to do with seeing real poverty up close for a first time, with the realization of how blessed we are in America. Another part is getting to know people who live in very different circumstances but share the need for Christian message and service. Some of the impact is just realizing how "alive" Christianity can be in other places.

As the movement grows, congregations have increasing opportunities to send a mission team of their own or to join some other church's team. A systematic way of presenting short-term mission trips done by Lutherans has not emerged yet. M.O.S.T Ministries (Mission Opportunities Short Term) in Ann Arbor is well organized and continues to expand mission opportunities to many parts of the world (www.most-ministries.org).

LIMINALITY

A new term is coming into usage to describe what happens when people get involved in many of the ministries discussed in this chapter. It is *liminality*, from the Latin word for "threshold." We have it in English to describe advertising that is "subliminal," below the threshold of perception.

Offering liminal, or threshold, experiences is a great way to help individual Christians move along in their personal spiritual journeys. When they are at the edge of past experience and starting to perceive new experiences, they are likely to discover realignments of their own priorities and commitments. When this happens in the context of Christian effort used by the Holy Spirit, the result can be truly called spiritual transformations.

The apostle Paul calls Christians to "be transformed into the Lord's likeness with ever increasing glory, which comes from the Lord, who is the Spirit" (2 Corinthians 3:18). Good ministry helps participants not only to reach such threshold points but also to recognize and discuss biblically what is happening.

Paul's ministry was all about building up congregations that transform the lives of their members. Such church transformation begins with individuals transformed by the Holy Spirit. Spiritually transformed individuals bring about transformational churches that in turn transform more participants. This kind of change is the goal of builder ministry.

QUESTIONS FOR DISCUSSION

1. How well does "the fellowship builder's toolbox" help you think about varieties of church ministries?

2. Where have you heard the Word of God especially well communicated?

3. How do you see the difference between sermons as proclamation or as communication?

4. Do you prefer to hear lectionary preaching or topical preaching?

5. Are preaching and celebrating the Sacraments well balanced in your congregation?

6. What are your thoughts on the tensions between contemporary worship and traditional worship?

7. Where have you shared prayer with others?

8. With which of the twelve spiritual disciplines outlined by Richard Foster do you have experience?

9. What is your experience with small-group ministry?

10. Have you ever done a spiritual renewal weekend? What do you know about them?

11. Have you ever been on a short-term mission trip, and if so, what was your experience?

PART III: RELATIONSHIPS

6

Cultivating Soil for the Holy Spirit

What makes ministry in the body of Christ special—and different from any other human endeavor? Without a moment of hesitation the apostle Paul would answer, dependence on the power of the Holy Spirit. That answer is true today, too, whether or not it is well recognized by those who lead modern Christian congregations.

In Luke's version of the ascension, Jesus tells his disciples not first to go but rather first to wait—"wait until you receive power when the Holy Spirit comes on you." Then they should go and be witnesses. The power for their witness will be the Holy Spirit.

The 1900s were the century for rediscovery of the Holy Spirit in the worldwide Christian church. Spirit-filled believers launched a variety of Pentecostal church bodies, which remain today the fastest growing churches around the world. Those who stayed within mainline church bodies are called charismatics.

Long-established church bodies have been rightfully cautious about recognizing the Spirit's work beyond the reliable established use of the means of Word and Sacraments. Jesus' teaching to Nicodemus that the Spirit is like an unpredictable wind (John 3:5–8) proves difficult to incorporate into the stable affairs of village churches.

Yet one has to wonder whether long-established church bodies have gone too far in the direction of losing reliance on the Holy Spirit. Too often the Spirit has been displaced by reliance on organization and managerial techniques to guide the work of churches, especially in the second half of the twentieth century, as businesses, social agencies and governments took on more refined managerial techniques for conducting their operations. Schools of administration emerged and their enrollments exploded.

I myself am a product of one of those graduate schools of business administration. I have served on many committees and task forces, trying to figure out how to get congregations and denominational offices to be better at what they want to do. Twenty years ago I co-wrote *Pastoral Administration: Integrating Ministry and Management in the Church.*[1] Part of being an expert on something is knowing not only what this specialty *can do* but also and especially what it *cannot do*. Organizational and administrative techniques cannot generate the special energy that makes Christian churches unique and effective in their own way.

Decades ago, another organizational specialist called the Presbyterian church to account for its almost total inattention to the Holy Spirit. Citing the prophet

Ezekiel's image of the Spirit as the wheel within the wheels of a chariot of living creatures, Richard G. Hutcheson, Jr. observed that all the wheels put into motion by church organizations would not go far without the wheel of the Holy Spirit that gives the church its unique identity and power.[2] He offered chapters of illustrations of its absence from his work with the General Assembly of the Presbyterian Church, U.S. His insights offer partial explanation for the decades of decline of mainline denominations.

Congregations and denominations that are in decline typically do not have just an organizational problem. Theirs is a spiritual problem. The organization might be better fine tuned, but little will come of it without recognition and dependence on the energy the Holy Spirit imparts.

THE HOLY SPIRIT IS KEY
TO CHURCH LIFE AND WORK

The apostle Paul knew very well that the Holy Spirit is key to the life and work of a Christian congregation. Hear from him directly:

My message and my preaching were not with wise and persuasive words, but with a demonstration of the Spirit's power, so that your faith might not rest on men's wisdom but on God's power. (1 Corinthians 2:4)

Don't you know that you yourselves are God's temple and that God's Spirit lives within you? (1 Corinthians 3:16)

You show that you are a letter from Christ, the result of our ministry, written not with ink but with the Spirit of the living God, not on tablets of stone but on tablets of human hearts. (2 Corinthians 3:3)

[God] has made us competent as ministers of a new covenant—not of the letter but of the Spirit; for the letter kills, but the Spirit gives life. (2 Corinthians 3:6)

In [Christ] the whole building is joined together and rises to become a holy temple in the Lord. And in him you too are being built together to become a dwelling in which God lives by his Spirit. (Ephesians 2:21, 22)

In the twelfth chapter of his letter to the Corinthians, Paul pulls together the various pieces of his theology applied to the life and work of a congregation.

No one can say, "Jesus is Lord," except by the Holy Spirit. There are different kinds of gifts, but the same Spirit. There are different kinds of service, but the same Lord. There are different kinds of working, but the same God works all of them in all men. Now to each one the manifestation of the Spirit is given for the common good.

This twelfth chapter of 1 Corinthians contains much more of Paul's teaching on the gifts of the Holy Spirit. More about that shortly.

MODELS OF THE CHURCH

Understandings of the role of the Holy Spirit in churches can be increased by identifying alternatives that do not feature the Spirit.

One of the classics of church analysis is *Models of the Church* by Avery Dulles.[3] He distinguishes five models adopted and used—knowingly or unknowingly—by Christian churches in understanding themselves and what they should be doing.

Church as institution. This is the official position of Roman Catholic doctrine. It is the default position of many Protestant congregations that have not cultivated ways for the Holy Spirit to keep enlivening them. Many declining churches lower their expectations to just keeping their organization going for another few years.

Church as sacrament. Here sacrament is used as symbol, and the model refers to the range of symbols that ministers use as signs of God's presence. At a minimum, baptism and the Lord's Supper are symbols of God's forgiving action. Lutherans believe they are more. Other symbols range from vestments to window design to processional objects. Statements of doctrine are officially called the symbols of a faith. With this understanding, the job of ministers is to keep the symbols before the people. This orientation has grown among Protestants as the liturgical movement emerged in the 1960s–80s. This orientation, however, assumes the presence of a strong fellowship of believers who are looking for reminders of their faith. It does not fit well when the task is the more basic one of first building up the fellowship of a congregation.

Church as herald. Some churches focus so much on the necessary task of witnessing in the community and world that they put little thought and effort into the other basics of a congregation's life in Christ: worship, discipleship, and service. This happens sometimes among crusade-oriented Baptists.

Church as servant. This model, like the herald, elevates one function of a congregation almost to the exclusion of the others. Here a church defines its purpose primarily by the needs it intends to meet in the community beyond itself. Liberal mainline church bodies tend in that direction, as they organize their ministries primarily around issues of promoting peace and justice.

Church as mystical community. While "mystical," as used by Avery Dulles, is not a word used often among Protestants, the same point can be made by understanding a congregation as a spiritual community, a community where the Holy Spirit is working—often in ways beyond human understanding—on the shared life of church members. Such a Spirit-driven church takes seriously all the functions that go with being the body of Christ: worship, discipleship, service, and witness. Fellowship is not a fifth function; it's the basic sharing that expresses itself in the four directions just listed.

This fifth model best fits Reformation teachings on the church as spiritual communion—"the Holy Spirit, the holy catholic church, the communion of saints" in the words of the Apostles' Creed. It is the Holy Spirit who precipitates the transformations involved in building up a lively congregation where all sorts of growth occur.

But the Spirit does so in his own time and way. Much to the frustration of church leaders over the centuries, we cannot plan or control the Spirit. He is like the wind which blows as it will. But we can invite him. We can look for evidence of his work and try to get in step with what he is doing.

LOOKING FOR THE HOLY SPIRIT

Let Martin Luther show us where to look: "The Holy Spirit has called me by the Gospel, enlightened me with his gifts, sanctified and kept me in the true faith; even as he calls, gathers, enlightens, and sanctifies the whole Christian Church on earth."[4]

Wherever someone is encountering Christ's call to follow and is hearing the good news of grace in Christ, there is the Holy Spirit at work. Where a present follower is participating in that encounter through personal witness and life, there is the Spirit in abundance.

Wherever presentations of the Word bring greater insights and illumination to someone, there is the Holy Spirit at work, especially so when greater understanding is awakened in the heart.[5]

Wherever a believer's new life in Christ becomes stronger and more evident, there is the Holy Spirit at work. Look for him working this outcome especially through means of "the mutual conversation and consolation of brethren," in Luther's phrase.[6]

Wherever a person is considering whether or not to attend church on a Sunday morning and feels the tug to do so, there is the Holy Spirit at work, and especially so when relationships to others in the fellowship help bring that affirmative response.

Wherever two or three come together in the name of Christ, there he is in a special way through the Holy Spirit (Matthew 18:20; Philippians 1:19). Look for the Spirit's work in improved relationships within a congregation and beyond it.

Wherever there is special boldness, or wisdom, or determination among Christians, there is the Holy Spirit in special ways. Luke, the writer of the Gospel and Acts, describes followers with such characteristics as being "filled with the Holy Spirit" (Acts 4:31; 6:3, 5, 8; 11:24). This description can be applied today to church members recognized as having special wisdom and courage. The Spirit also brings freedom, and his work can be seen whenever a follower of Christ finds new levels of joy and peace through release from guilt and expectations of perfection (2 Corinthians 3:17).

Wherever Christians come together with special energy and sing with gusto and intensity, there is the Holy Spirit (Colossians 3:16). "Spirit team" is a new name for cheerleaders at sporting events. When God's Spirit touches human spirits, the joy can be like that of a high-energy event happening among those gathered in the name of Christ.

Consider this viewpoint of Paul for spotting the Holy Spirit: The hallmark of the Spirit is newness. God promises the Spirit will put a *new* heart and a *new* spirit into his people (Ezekiel 36:16). Paul tells the Romans that the Spirit brings *new* ways different from living by rules. He tells the Corinthians that *new* life-giving relationships come through the *new* covenant of the Spirit (Romans 7:6; 2 Corinthians 3:6).

Some would understand the new life brought by the Spirit as a one-time event—at conversion. But Lutherans understand it is a frequent, even daily, process of drowning out the old nature in us through repentance and letting the new nature come forth and arise. Being made new again—renewal—is the Holy Spirit's work. The Spirit's way is movement, not status quo.

Paul explains to the Corinthians that the Holy Spirit transforms us into Christ-likeness with the movement of "ever-increasing glory" (2 Corinthians 3:18). We are to be thus transformed by the renewing of our minds (Romans 12:2). The Spirit does that with individuals. But he also can do so with congregations. The work of getting members aligned with Christ and with each other for ministries that build up the body of Christ should have the goal of reaching to the very heights of the fullness of Christ. Whatever an individual Christian or a congregation might be reaching now, there is more the Spirit wants to give and do. Settling for existing conditions is not the preferred outcome for life in the Spirit.

CELEBRATING TRANSFORMATIONS

Sometimes the Spirit scores big in the life of a person or a congregation. We can call those transformations. It is good to spot these when they occur and to give thanks.

Transformation is a strong word that is too frequently trivialized. It means a basic change in the nature of something. *Transformation* is from the Latin. Its Greek equivalent is *metamorphosis*, a term we use today to describe what happens when a caterpillar changes into a butterfly.

Transformation happens in a big way when an individual's encounter with Christ brings a whole new self-understanding and lifestyle. It happens when someone comes back from a mission trip and says it was a life-changing experience. It happens in a little way when a Christian reaches a higher level of peace about conflicting and confusing demands being made upon her. Little transformations look like steps made toward greater maturity in Christ-like living.

Congregations, too, have transformations. This can happen in big ways when members in conflict reach a new and higher level of peace and cooperation, especially when church leaders have sought the guidance of the Spirit. With a keen eye, one can see this higher unity emerge once in a while in meetings. It happens when a new commitment to a mission outreach brings a basic change in a church's self-understanding and energy. Sometimes it happens with a well-processed commitment to a building construction project. Putting up physical buildings is a well-known good approach to fellowship building.

With Spirit-guided experience, church leaders can learn to see the Holy Spirit at work in many aspects of a congregation's life. Looking for the Spirit, they can try new ways to receive his impact in a church. Then they are on the way to truly distinctive Christian leadership. When asked, God does promise to send his Spirit. With the Spirit comes new human energy and commitment. Then a congregation can get to the task of organizing it better.

Some congregations can look back at their history and recognize a certain point when their church took on new direction and energy. The Holy Spirit was at work in fresh ways. With tongues of fire as a symbol for the Spirit, these can be truly called igniter events. It might be a construction project, but could also happen with the coming of a new pastor, or response to a new community challenge, or the welcome arrival of new leaders. Just as Spirit-driven human transformations cannot be scheduled, so also congregational igniter events cannot be humanly programmed. They happen in God's timing. But like individual Christians, congregations can pray for the Spirit, prepare themselves, and consider the sorts of activities being used well by the Spirit in other congregations. Then when the wind of the Spirit does blow, they should be prepared to work extra hard at welcoming and focusing the new energy.

Celebrating special spiritual transformations does not deny the Spirit's presence in ordinary church life. Being "filled with the Spirit" does not imply the alternative of no presence. The Spirit does bring patience, gentleness and meekness as well as boldness and courage.

And he brings newness. That comes with the challenge to become more Christlike in the future than at present. The status quo might be great. But there can be so much more in the Spirit.

CULTIVATING CHURCH LIFE FOR THE HOLY SPIRIT

How does one get the Holy Spirit more involved in a church's life? As with all things of the Spirit, the process starts with prayer. Recall Jesus' teaching on prayer with the memorable phrase, Ask and it will be given to you; seek and you will find; knock and the door will be opened to you. Less well recognized is that four verses later in the Luke account is the completion of that promise: "If you know how to give good gifts to your children, how much more will your Father in heaven give the Holy Spirit to those who ask him!" (Luke 11:13).

We can pray that the Father send his Holy Spirit. Like Zacchaeus, we can figuratively climb a sycamore tree so that we are more visibly in his way. Zacchaeus was a wealthy short man in need. He wanted to know more about who this Jesus is. So he climbed a sycamore tree to better see—and to be seen. Jesus did indeed spot him and immediately invited himself to stay at Zacchaeus' house. How do we get Jesus to stay in the house of our hearts through the Holy Spirit? We purposely put ourselves where the Spirit can work on us.

We can put ourselves in a better position by becoming active rather than passive in seeking him; we can read the Scriptures and pray regularly rather than sporadically. We can spend more time with other Christians who are open to his ways and who are committed to reliable means by which he comes: Word and Sacraments. Luther called the mutual conversation and consolation of the brethren a means of grace.[7] We can put ourselves where some kind of response to the Word is expected by regular spiritual disciplines, especially disciplines like tithing that challenge us to rely on the Spirit to stretch our faith.

We have no immediate control over the Spirit, who comes when and where he wills. But we can prepare the ground to better receive him when he does come. We can cultivate church life so the Holy Spirit has an easier time getting through. We can be better hosts for the Spirit.

Cultivation, of course, fits in well with Paul's image of the congregation as a garden. More is involved in growing healthy plants than to put down seed and to water. In the middle of the growing season, my farmer uncles in Illinois would attach hoe-like devices to the tractor and break up the soil by driving between the rows of corn. They were cultivating. Breaking up the ground serves to let more water and nutrients through to the roots and also to displace and kill weeds.

How do you cultivate church life? When the surface of the soil of life together becomes hardened and encrusted over time, you break it up by presenting alternatives to old well-established church patterns. You try new approaches to Bible study. You try new, attention-holding illustrations in the sermon—perhaps a drama or dramatic reading. You find ways to highlight stories of personal change. You lead the way to several new mission commitments.

To Paul, the movement of building up church life was important so that a congregation could reach higher toward the fullness of Christ. You cannot expect much church movement forward by doing the same old things the same old ways with the same people. Building up inherently involves change by bringing building material together in new forms—by bringing new challenges to a gathered body of Christ.

PERSPECTIVES ON GOD'S MULTIFACETED WISDOM

Paul, the fellowship builder, describes the job of the church as presenting the multifaceted wisdom of God (Ephesians 3:10). Think of a diamond in a ring. It has many cuts, or facets, on its surface; the more facets, the greater the value of the diamond. It's the facets that cause the diamond to sparkle, to "bling," as movement brings different angles into the perspective of the beholder.

A basic task of the ministry of preaching and teaching is to turn the diamond through various angles to show different facets of God's wisdom. Jesus was an expert at this. He described himself as the bread of life, the light of the world, the good shepherd, the gate for the sheep, the resurrection and life, the way, the vine.

But there is another way to see different facets. That is to move the person who is doing the beholding so that he or she sees God's wisdom in new and different personal contexts, thus breaking up he soil. In the pew on Sunday is one viewpoint. In a discussion Bible class at church is another. Meeting regularly in a home for shared prayer and Bible study is another context. So can be worshipping in a gym with new songs and music, committing to a service project, seeking personal confession and absolution, going on a weekend renewal retreat, hearing the testimonies of others, accepting the challenge of tithing income, and going on a mission trip to see God at work in people very different from those at home.

Working to move members from passive receptors of the Word to active spreaders and appliers of the Word can accomplish a lot of soil cultivation.

Think of such changed contexts as additional opportunities for the Spirit to bring new insights and growth among those interacting together in the name of Christ. Think of planning such events as raising the sail on a ship. When the Spirit blows, the ship moves in ways that can be very exciting. But just because the sail is up does not mean that the wind will blow. On the other hand, if the wind does blow but the sail is not up, then opportunities for Spirit-led encounters have been lost. Determination to move the ship of congregational life is basic to builder ministry. Such determination usually means trying out new ministry offerings, like an Alpha Course Bible discussion series, or involving members in nursing home ministries, or a Wednesday evening study and interaction time for both children and adults.

Experienced builder ministers report that perhaps one out of three of their program initiatives work, that is, attract enough people to make the effort worth continuing. The decision to give up should be made only after several attempts. Waiting for the wind of the Holy Spirit to blow can become very discouraging. But, nevertheless, maybe a new sail at a different time might yield exciting results. If you have not had many ministry initiatives that went nowhere in a congregation, you are probably are not trying hard enough. The apostle Paul never suggested that ministry is easy.

In letters to each of his congregations, Paul the builder challenged them again and again to some higher level of fellowship sharing expressed as greater love or unity or witness or offerings. Not everyone likes to be challenged. It makes many people uncomfortable, just like change does. Shepherd ministers are inclined to respond to discomforts by avoiding challenges. Their instinct is to comfort by maintaining old patterns. But builder ministers see the offering of well-thought-out challenges as basic to their calling. Raising up such challenges can be thought of as designing experiences for congregational participants that anticipate the Spirit acting through the Word.

RELEASING THE HOLY SPIRIT

Just planning variety and freshness in worship services can be a very demanding task for a minister. Add to that the planning of many different context-changing events and programs, and ministry can quickly become overwhelming. And it certainly is so for a shepherd minister who wants to be the hub around which all congregational relationships and activities occur. Such limits are why broadening the understanding of ministry is so important. To multiply ministries in a church is why Paul taught that everyone is a minister. This starting point means the task for leaders is to get all of them into alignment for building up their fellowship. This job today inevitably means giving special attention to planning, organizing and supervising their congregation's ministry-affirming fellowship.

A common problem of shepherd churches today is finding enough people to fill all the board and committee positions that are supposed to plan and carry out activities of the congregation. "We can't get people to do anything," is a common complaint of shepherd ministers.

Builder Paul would not be sympathetic. He had a different view of the Holy Spirit. He was convinced the Spirit was ready to provide the necessary energy. His practice was 180 degrees opposite that of many churches today that look for any members willing to be fitted into a box of assignments. In 1 Corinthians 12 he stated his assumption that each member is given a manifestation of the Spirit to do something for the common good of the congregation. Such a gift often looks like a person with a passion. Leaders just need to identify that spiritual gift and help the individual put it into action. That sort of administration of God's differing gifts is how the apostle Peter, too, did ministry. He told his readers, "Each should use whatever gift he has received to serve others, faithfully administering God's grace in its various forms" (1 Peter 4:10). A spiritual gift is not just a person's talent, but a talent that an individual is being moved by the Spirit to put to use in the congregation, be it teaching a class, hosting a small group, consoling the sick, encouraging teens, greeting visitors or witnessing to their faith at work.

This dynamic approach to church leadership is definitely a break from the traditions of European-based church bodies. In that model, congregations were not expected to do much beyond receiving and then supporting the ministry of the ordained pastor. Yet the teaching is so clear in the writings of Peter and of course Paul, who developed this thought also in the twelfth chapter to the Romans. Like the builder concept itself, one wonders why it was overlooked in centuries of pastoral practice.

Many different inventories of gifts are available for congregations that want to do spiritual gift administration. None of them pretends to have scientific value. They are basically meant as a jumping-off place for self-discovery and discussions of what individuals can contribute—beyond supporting the work of the ordained minister. The individual can recognize the Spirit's movement within when he or she enjoys doing that ministry. A congregation can recognize the Spirit's movement in that member when he or she does this effort well.

The task of church leadership is dramatically changed by this starting assumption of the Spirit's presence and movement within each participant. Instead of cajoling members to take on a responsibility—often with the assurance they will not have to do much—the challenge now is to find enough opportunities for everyone to put to use his or her contribution that the Spirit is moving them to do for the common good. This is what it means to get church members aligned for ministries that build up the body of Christ. One can talk about "unleashing" the saints by encouraging and supporting them as they work out what the Spirit may be leading them to offer.

This newly rediscovered starting point for congregational life clearly leads toward seeing the builder's task, including that of the ordained, as contractors who find and engage the many who do the hands-on carpentry ministries of a congregation.

This very Scriptural perspective also calls for much more attention to the architectural demands of builder ministry. Instead of relying on tradition to determine what a congregation will do in the future based on what it has done in the past, a builder minister will try to cast a compelling, energizing vision that best utilizes the circumstances and gifts of that particular congregation as it moves toward reaching the very heights of the fullness of Christ in that place. It might be a vision to minister better to young families by starting a preschool. Or it might be to get members deeper in the Word by having a "Year of the Bible" with a wide range of special offerings. Or it might be to become more mission minded in the neighborhood by developing an Hispanic ministry. Or it might be to focus on world mission by adopting a missionary family in Africa or some other distant land.

This kind of architectural ministry can be very exciting.

CAUTIONS

What I have described here as glimpses of the Holy Spirit does not pretend to be a full theology of the Spirit. It is, though, certainly consistent with orthodox Reformation thinking about the Spirit.

Sometimes the Spirit moves in spectacular ways even today as he did in Paul's day. Some people do receive now and then the gift of speaking in tongues, for instance, and sometimes otherwise-unexplainable healings happen. To deny these possibilities would be a strange reading of the biblically authoritative teaching of Paul, especially in 1 Corinthians 14:5, where he commends speaking in tongues and then describes the circumstances where it is best done.

For shepherd ministers and congregations, such unusual manifestations of the Spirit can seem like anything but a gift to their life together, and their reaction may be to force out what they see as disturbances. Builder ministers are inclined, however, to see it for what it *could* be: fresh energy provided by the Spirit along with all the other gifts to the common good. The builder's challenge is wisely to guide this gift, along with all others, to build up the fellowship, rather than to let it be torn down.

Some ask rightfully whether any spirited activity in a Christian congregation is evidence of the Holy Spirit versus some other spirit. Paul would answer that if the fellowship gathered around Word and Sacrament is built up, the Holy Spirit is probably behind it (2 Corinthians 3:6). Others might observe that signs of enthusiasm in a church might be just the same kind of human spirit cheerleaders work on. Indeed, the Holy Spirit does touch human spirit. Paul would observe that you have to look for evidence of the Spirit through eyes of faith, which in turn are only given by the Spirit. This is a circular argument that does not impress human wisdom. Paul would say, so be it.

If you are committed to Christian ministry, it is better to invite, expect, and celebrate the Holy Spirit than to overlook him or take him for granted. The alternative is to be just another human organization in competition with so many others.

QUESTIONS FOR DISCUSSION

1. How have you recognized movement of the Holy Spirit in church life?

2. Do you see the decline of church bodies more as an organizational issue or as a spiritual issue?

3. What do you see as ways to have more of the Spirit's movement in your personal and also your church life?

4. Which of the five models of church squares best with your understanding before this study: institution, sacrament, herald, servant, or spiritual communion?

5. What is your reaction to the suggestions on where to look to find evidence of the Holy Spirit's action in normal church life?

6. Have you experienced or witnessed "transformation" in individual Christian life or in a congregation's life?

7. How is the soil of your church's life cultivated for the Holy Spirit's work among you?

8. Can you think of additional ways to cultivate the soil?

9. What is your experience with "spiritual gifts administration"?

10. What is your reaction to the claim that "You have to look for the Spirit through eyes of faith, which in turn are only given by the Spirit"?

7

Sharing Experiences and Feelings

"The peace of God, which passeth all understanding, keep your hearts and minds through Christ Jesus."

I grew up hearing that passage from Philippians 4:7 at the end of every sermon. Later I realized it is the prescribed sermon ending in *The Lutheran Hymnal* of 1942. Other versions say "the peace which surpasses all human understanding." The familiarity of regular usage unfortunately can gloss over special significance.

Since those days, I did a PhD in Organizational Behavior and have been a member of the American Psychological Association for 36 years. I learned to see a whole new meaning. Such peace is the ultimate outcome of a profound religious experience. Through his dramatic conversion, Paul certainly knew what that peace meant, and he wished all could share it.

William James, in his *Varieties of Religious Experience* of 1902, gave classic expression to religious experience. He highlights descriptions such as "an incomparable feeling of happiness which is connected with the near presence of God's spirit," and "a sense of a presence, strong, and at the same time soothing, which hovers over me."

There is now an extensive literature on the psychology of religious experience.[1] The categories, descriptions, and theories vary widely. Experiences can be confirming, or responsive, or ecstatic, or revelational.[2] Offering terms that sometimes appear in worship literature, Rudolf Otto considers experience of the holy as a consciousness wholly other than rational (*mysterium*) and distinguishes between consciousness of awe, majesty, energy (*tremendum*) and consciousness of peace, perfect love, mystery, salvation (*fascinans*).[3] Those who have not had a religious experience have a hard time understanding what others are talking about. All agree that those who have such an experience need images and a vocabulary to express it, and that vocabulary differs among religions and church bodies.

Such experiences are not rare occurrences found only among scattered "mystics." Sociologist Andrew Greeley (a reputable pollster and a Roman Catholic priest) reported in 1974 that his surveys of the general population found that 39% of respondents could report an overwhelming religious experience. In later surveys he found that reports of religious experience had increased on four indicators about 5%–10% between 1973 and 1988.[4] George Gallup reported in 1989 that 43% of respondents to his surveys affirm they had "been aware of, or influenced by, a presence or a power—whether they called it God or not—which is different from their everyday selves."[5]

This literature covers the broad human experience of that "something other." As Paul wished for the Philippians, it certainly can happen to today's Christians. It can even happen to Lutherans. In a random survey (418 returns) of prayer practices among members of 105 congregations of The Lutheran Church—Missouri Synod, I found that 55% regularly experience "a deep sense of peace during prayer," and 45% regularly feel "the strong presence of God during prayer."[6] You would never guess these high percentages from interactions within traditional Lutheran church culture, which often seems to discourage such discussion of feelings. A vocabulary for spiritual feelings and experience does not come easily.

Sociologist Andrew Greeley, by the way, found that half the 39% who reported having had a religious experience never told anyone because they were so intimidated by their culture. We can ask whether traditional church cultures are similarly intimidating, and at what expense. Only after some discussion with a young woman in my church planting effort did she relate a life-changing, near-death experience in a serious automobile accident. She was searching for what it meant but did not think a church could help her.

There is a tension between religious experience as reported by a random sample of people or described by psychologists and the peace that passes all understanding that Paul wrote about. The peace Paul knew from his conversion onward was the peace of God that keeps hearts and minds in Jesus Christ. But Christians cannot lay exclusive claim to religious experience. We trust that the peace brought by the Holy Spirit can be even more profound than other versions. The point here is that we can help the Spirit accomplish such peace in others when we are more willing to share our own experiences.

EXPERIENCE, BELIEVE, BELONG

The reason for highlighting religious experience is that it seems key to the greater success believer-baptizing church bodies have for building new members into their church community. Their sequence of movement inward typically starts with helping them find and talk about some new Experience they had in an encounter with Christ. Then comes teaching the basics of Belief, followed by Belonging in the community.

The sequence for infant-baptizing churches, as described in chapter 1, is the opposite: first Belong as a child, then Believe at confirmation, and then have an Experience—maybe. The challenge is to become more comfortable recognizing and talking about religious experiences. Of course, experiences of the Holy Spirit moving in one's life are not ours humanly to give. But we can cultivate the soil to be more receptive of the Spirit not only for ourselves but also for others. Certainly we can get better at communicating the kind of experiences that one out of two Lutherans say they have in the context of prayer.

CONVERSION

The defining experience in believer-baptizing churches is conversion, also called being born again. With an understanding of the Sacrament of Baptism different from what we Lutherans confess, they see it as a public statement of that conversion experience, preferably identified by time and place.

Sharing personal born-again stories is a delightful part of Evangelical church culture. When done formally they become testimonies. As stories of relationships, they are easy to listen to and identify with. Shared informally, they can stimulate conversation and lead to other descriptions of what God is doing in their personal lives today. Where in traditional church cultures one would usually find social small talk, in Evangelical church culture, one is more likely to hear God talk. All this is a plus for reaching out and building up relationships with others, especially new participants. It flows from a focus on personal spiritual experiences, a willingness to share these, and a vocabulary for putting them into words. Such God talk moves beyond the big "before and after" story on to accounts of "What God did in my life this week," or expressions of thanks for a special blessing, or requests for prayers for one situation or another.

Studies of conversion point out that the confirmation and support of others are needed for an individual spiritual commitment to be lasting. It is the fellowship that offers the vocabulary and affirmation to explain the individual's experience. H. Newton Malony observes that all conversion has its sociodynamics. He concludes, "Whereas inner decision may be a first step, it must be followed by attachment to a social group for real-life change to happen."[7]

The culture of a church makes a big difference.

INFANT-BAPTIZED HANDICAP

Those of us who were baptized as infants usually do not have conversion stories to tell. Raised as children in a Christian context of home and church, we have been Christians as long as we can remember. This is typically not a very exciting story. Most of us do not have a dramatic "before and after" experience.

The blessings and confidence of a Christian upbringing can themselves be a barrier to building relationships with others whose background is different. We sometimes inadvertently communicate a tone of superiority. If we are heavily involved in our church culture, we often don't even meet the unchurched, and when we do, we often don't now how to talk with them winsomely.

So often we start with assumptions and experiences that are very different from theirs. We assume that all believe in God, that all sin, that all need to be saved, and that all worry about heaven and hell. In our increasingly secular society, those beliefs are no longer widespread. Learning how to better communicate experiences—not just doctrine—would be a worthy change in infant-baptizing church cultures. Our society does have a willingness to hear stories of how personal beliefs have made a difference in quality of life and how relationships in a church fellowship have brought peace and joy. It is one thing to say Christian beliefs are important. A better witness is to show how even life-long Christian faith has made a difference in one's life at a specific time with a specific concern or problem.

AWAKENING

An appropriate vocabulary does exist in the heritage of Lutheran churches, but it has fallen out of use in the past century or so. The key concept is "awakening." These would be times in one's personal life when the relationship with Christ took on new and deeper meaning.

The dominant leader in eighteenth century Lutheranism in America, Henry Muhlenberg, would ask candidates for ministry to discuss their first awakening. This is a great question. What was it like when your infant baptism took on new meaning? The first awakening suggests more than one in a lifetime. The frequency and intensity varies from person to person as the Holy Spirit does his work individually. Muhlenberg's question implies that it is hard to be an effective and wise Christian leader with just knowledge that does not have a base of spiritual experience.

Awakenings happen when head knowledge is transformed into heart experience and conviction. Sometimes this happens at eighth grade confirmation. I had my first awakening about that age in the form of a growing conviction to study for the ministry. The apostle Paul's admonishment in Romans 12:2 to offer our bodies as living sacrifices pleasing to God had a big impact on me. For some, the first awakening comes later, perhaps in college or at a time of intense stress. In an Evangelical culture, they would be led to describe this as a conversion. A church culture that explains it as an awakening seems better, if only for expecting subsequent additional awakenings in the course of a lifetime. Otherwise, the person's conversion or being born again in theory happens only once.

I have enjoyed discussions with Lutheran church members when I probed for something like a spiritual awakening in their personal lives. For some, finding and talking about that comes easily. Others may struggle with a level of personal reflection they are not used to. But usually something emerges, and often it was at a time of the death of someone close. Asking for a "mountaintop experience" can sometimes trigger awareness of a time of spiritual growth. Some respond well to an inquiry about a personal "epiphany" they might have had.

A contemporary framework I have found helpful is offered by Janet Hagberg and Robert Guelich in *The Critical Journey: Stages in the Life of Faith*.[8] The authors distinguish between the stage of initial recognition of God, moving on to the life of discipleship, and then the productive life of ministry. Of six stages, Stage 4 is the journey inward that comes with a "wall experience." Hitting the wall is an intense time of personal failure to accomplish something very important one intended to do with his or her own ability and power. Often the Spirit can use that to produce a profound surrender to God that offers a glimpse of the peace beyond human understanding that Paul was talking about. The authors note that most on the spiritual journey cannot understand a stage further than one beyond where they are at the time.

I had a wall experience the second winter of the church plant effort when frustration with a lack of growth and a serious illness combined to produce a bleak February. My high-visibility church plant felt like a failure, and I would have to move the family on to yet one more place with a ministry less dependent on the planter's personality. The Holy Spirit used that time to open my eyes to new spiritual insights and to rearrange my priorities around God's agenda, not my own. Jesus' challenge in Mark 8:34 took on new meaning: "If anyone would come after me, he must deny himself and take up his cross, and follow me. For whoever wants to save his life will lose it, but whoever loses his life for me and for the gospel will save it." With acceptance of loss came peace. A fascination with prayer also emerged. I am so thankful God still had plenty of life and work for me.

WHY NOT

Infant-baptizing church bodies with a long history have a track record of resistance to highlighting personal spiritual experiences. Why is that?

In a phrase, fear of going too far.

1. At Luther's time, the *Schwaermeri* or enthusiasts went too far in interpreting their personal experiences of God as empowering them to announce new teachings and to pursue an agenda of overturning what they thought was ungodly in church and state. The destructive Peasants' Revolt of 1525 was a soul-searing time for Luther and made him much more aware of how sinfulness can contaminate personal experiences.

The corrective is always to test an inner experience against the objective Word. Hate and destructive behavior is not from God. From the Holy Spirit comes that which builds up a fellowship.

2. In the more recent time of the charismatic movement of the 1960s and 70s, those who received special experiences of the Holy Spirit, perhaps in the form of speaking in tongues or miraculous healings, became a source of serious divisiveness in congregation after congregation. Too often they conveyed, even inadvertently, a sense of spiritual superiority over church members who had not received those particular gifts.

The corrective is to stress the diverse ways the Holy Spirit touches lives and works his way. The constant temptation is to make one's own experience prescriptive for somebody else's experience. The serious study of Christian spirituality, gathered from writings about experiences over two thousand years, stresses that there is no one best way to seek and be found by the Holy Spirit beyond reliance on his Word. Personality differences are significant. Studies published in 1987 and 1991 spawned other research showing how different expressions of prayer and spirituality are more effective for some personalities than for others.[9] The Myers Briggs Type Indicator was used to distinguish types of personality.

3. Too often those who focus on the emotions of their spiritual experience are inclined to judge their relationship with God on the basis of those emotions. The pastoral concern is what happens when those emotions lessen or go away or even turn negative. Does that mean God has abandoned such a person or that the person no longer has saving faith? The subtle temptation is to think that our feelings make us worthy of God's attention rather than to simply trust in his grace without any merit or worthiness on our part. Putting people in emotional situations where they are expected to make a decision for Christ is not wise shepherding. That shepherd concern remains one of the strengths of churches with long traditions.

The corrective is to stress the sequence of three Fs: Feelings come after Faith based on recognition of Fact. The fact is the objective truth of Scriptures. Faith simply trusts the fact of that promise. Feelings flow out of such trust.

A strength of the shepherd model is that its sequence of Belong, Believe, and Experience respects that sequence of Fs. But too often this comes at the expense of not recognizing and sharing the spiritual experiences that can more readily build up the relationships within a church's fellowship. The sequence of Experience, Believe, Belong is riskier because it might lose focus on the Facts of objective truth. But then any kind of building effort has risks of some sort. Wise pastoring will keep Experience linked with biblical Facts and Faith.

In his 1983 review of experience and faith in light of the charismatic movement, William Hordern offers this summary observation: "Luther in no way denied the reality of the inner sense of communion with God that the Christian experiences. Luther himself knew this experience and has many beautiful things to say about it. . . . His concern was not to discourage inner experience but to set it in the proper perspective."[10]

The expression of personal experiences is inherently subjective. Sometimes the phrases used can seem at odds with objective truth that God's Word teaches. Just proclaiming those objectives truths of doctrine is undoubtedly easier. Yet pastorally we should remain open to Luther's approach, which as Hordern notes, was not to deny or discourage inner experience but to provide perspective. The pastoral task in discussions with individuals is to teach and apply biblical interpretation. Sometimes when hearing someone's story, I might say something like, here is a better way to express that. Almost always they will accept the phrases I suggest as a better reflection of what they mean. What precious moments when someone shares his or her personal experience in their own words! Adding biblical perspective needs to be done with sensitivity.

FAITHFUL FEELINGS

Several times I have heard worship leaders wisely advise against trusting emotions that may be aroused in worship—"because it might just be a reaction to something you ate." Good advice. Poor theory.

Rene Descartes and Charles Darwin laid the foundation for non-cognitive theories of emotions that see them as just neurological reactions to bodily conditions. According to these theories, emotions are non-cognitive; physiological changes in the body produce particular emotions. Seldom are they noble or trustworthy.

But a larger school of psychologists in the last century have taken a cognitive approach; that is, they view thought, appraisal, and belief as central elements in emotions. Cognitive theory integrates emotion and intellect. Emotions are reactions to something perceived. They reveal whether someone sees the world or some aspect of it as threatening or welcoming, painful or pleasant. Change the perception and the emotions may change. This is the assumption behind most forms of therapy today. Perception and thus emotions are subject to reason and evaluation.[11]

In his book *Faithful Feelings*, Matthew Elliott maintains that theologians over the years have taken a non-cognitive approach. They tend to separate emotion and reason, which causes them to downplay the significance of emotions in the Christian life. A cognitive understanding would lead to greater appreciation of the positive emotions as an important part of the blessings God gives by way of the Holy Spirit through encounters with the Word, Christ Jesus.[12]

I have borrowed Elliott's title of Faithful Feelings for the heading of this section. He notes that in the New Testament the heart is a person's self and includes more than emotions. The heart is the place where faith takes root in both mind and emotion, as expressed in Paul's prayer for the Ephesians that "the eyes of your heart may be enlightened" (Ephesians 1:18). In Scripture, knowledge of a thing is greater than belief in its existence. Emotion, like love, can be commanded. Emotion cannot be changed by dwelling on the emotion itself, but it can be changed by dwelling on and changing the beliefs and evaluations that lie behind it.[13]

This little bit of theory helps to explain how the importance of emotions has been underappreciated in the work of Paul. He wrote frequently of the emotions that can build up relationships in the fellowships he was leading. These are not just the faith, hope, and love of 1 Corinthians 13. They include patience, kindness, goodness, faithfulness, gentleness, and self-control.

FRUIT OF THE SPIRIT

The fifth chapter to the Galatians is foundation-laying teaching for church building. The topic sentence urges believers to use their freedom in the Gospel to serve one another in love. He reminds them of how the desires of sinful nature are destructive to individuals and relationships. In contrast, "the fruit of the Spirit is love, joy, peace, patience, kindness, goodness, faithfulness, gentleness, and self-control."

These are emotions—certainly good ones to have, especially in life together. If some do not seem emotional, think of their opposite, like hate, sorrow, impatience. One can almost see the blood pressure rising in those who are seriously impatient. By my count, *love* shows up in Paul's letters twenty-seven times, *joy/rejoice* thirty-five times, and *peace* forty-one times.

Is Paul in effect just urging members to be nice to each other? What is special about that? Everybody would agree such encouragement is good. But these emotions are fruit of the *Holy Spirit*. Several verses earlier Paul teaches that these feelings come through living by the Spirit, or staying in step with the Spirit (Galatians 5:16). I think the *fruit* of the Spirit has been underappreciated in traditional churches as much as the *gifts* of the Spirit. This is because so much of the breadth of Biblical teaching on the Holy Spirit has been filtered out of routine church life over the centuries. The Holy Spirit's energy is not often prayed for and thus is often not evident. One good place to look for the Spirit's action is in the emotions of those gathered in the name of Christ who expect to grow in their spiritual maturity, and thus in their relational emotions. They bring enthusiasm for digging into the Bible and encouragement to each other in their personal spiritual journey.

Awakenings describe *big* movements of the Holy Spirit in one's life. The more we share them with others, the closer we feel to them. *Changed emotions* are *routine* fruit of the Spirit's work. They take on added significance when looked at in the context of life in Christ. Such valuable context can come through fellowship with other Christians. Minor victories over unwanted emotions can be shared and in turn stimulate additional productive God talk. "Let me tell you how I learned to be more patient with my children" can be a great conversation piece and relation builder.

A RELATIONSHIPS-ORIENTED CULTURE

My own personal observation is that talk about relationships and emotions seems to communicate especially well in contemporary society.

Bookstores have shelves of self-help books that sell well. Lots of people don't like the way they are and want to be better, usually in relationships. None of the self-help books work very well; otherwise there would not be so many. Paul teaches us that the cause of empty lives and damaged relationships is our sinful nature, and we can't do much to change ourselves. What a great opportunity for Christians to share the significance of life in Christ and how his Spirit can make a difference in the way we live, and how the Spirit can move us from a life that is all about me to a life all about God. Recognition of disturbing emotions and their effects is a great starting point for confessing sin, hearing absolution and anticipating the power of God to get better.

Another reflection of our changed American culture is that the persuasiveness of Biblical images for salvation in Christ has shifted in recent generations. For years I taught new members four images for salvation: In Romans 3:24, 25 Paul presents justification (the court scene), redemption (the slave market) and the sacrifice of atonement (Old Testament sacrifices). In 2 Corinthians 5 he focuses on reconciliation (being made friends with God). The question I then ask is which of these four images they find most helpful and persuasive for themselves personally. Consistently and by a significant margin the image of friendship with God is the favorite. They tend to see life as all about relationships.

For earlier generations the courtroom image had more appeal. Standing guilty before God and having Christ pay our fine was persuasive for understanding and sharing the role of Christ in human life. The alternative between heaven and hell had more intensity.

In general, eternal consequences are no longer so compelling in newer American generations. Of course justification, hell and heaven are Biblical truths and still need to be taught. They just don't connect they way they used to as a base for communicating the Gospel.

THE LIMITS OF GUILT

Not only do traditional images for communicating the Gospel not work as well, but also traditional ways of leading congregational life don't have the impact they used to. Guilt is simply not as persuasive a motivator as it used to be.

Shepherd pastors in shepherd congregations have had a lot of power to influence the behavior of members. As long as they stay within the familiar framework, shepherds can define what is good membership and what are the expectations for involvement. A reasonable number of participants will respond.

What these shepherds are often doing in actuality is appealing to a sense of guilt. Members care enough about their identity with a church body and about their involvement in a congregation that they let their behavior be influenced by the pastor's expectations. If they don't, they will feel guilty as lax church members. Such response helps fill committee positions, boost turnout at special events, and increase attendance on Christmas and Easter.

There are at least two disadvantages to relying on guilt as a technique of church leadership. One is that it brings only enough response to get off the hook of guilt. Once a minimum has been met, the motivation to do more is weak. Guilt seldom produces attractive, spiritual life-affirming liveliness.

The second problem with guilt is that it does not work well with people who have little loyalty to the congregation and its church body. Shepherd ministry assumes a preexisting community of participants who bring fellowship commitments with them. Take away that commitment and with it goes the guilt that brings willingness to be influenced in ways they would otherwise avoid.

Businesses speak about brand loyalty. Churches used to count on denominational loyalty. The discussion in chapter 3 of Robert Putnum's study on *Bowling Alone* demonstrated how such loyalty is in decline in America in all areas of life, including businesses and churches. Weakening loyalty is especially true for church bodies with a history of ethnic identity.

ALTERNATIVES

Without denominational loyalty, how do you lead a church? Welcome to world of ministry in urban and suburban churches today.

One alternative is to keep doing ministry as it has been done over the generations. Some people will respond, and some churches can continue for the foreseeable future.

To change is difficult for ministers. It involves risks. Will it work? Will the resistance be too strong? Do I have the skills? Will I still be faithful? The counterquestion that has to be faced is, Am I being faithful to a culture or to the necessary truths of this church? How important is it to reach out in new ways to those beyond the present congregation?

A different alternative is to copy somebody else's church culture. There are many wannabes out there, wanting to imitate the ways of a highly respected ministry, like that of Willow Creek Community Church. Seldom do they come out as well. Where a congregation is unusually healthy and growing, there you will usually find a special combination of leaders, people and ministry that builds on the strengths of a specific congregation with its leaders and its circumstances. Besides, why give up the many strengths of a culture of an infant-baptizing tradition?

The third alternative is to think like a builder who renovates houses, or to use Paul's image, who renovates the spiritual "temple" of a congregation gathered at a specific time and place. You don't tear it all down to start over again. You find the strengths to build up and accentuate. You recognize the weaknesses to be shored up or at least not overstressed. You add a "room" of a new worship service here, a new version of children's ministry there. You try a renewal weekend here and a mission trip there. You keep looking for what the Holy Spirit seems ready to bless then and there. You especially affirm individuals who seem to be led by the Spirit to step forward for a new ministry. You cultivate soil and lead prayer for the Holy Spirit to come with special energy for the people gathered together in this body of Christ.

The renovation of a spiritual temple and its church culture may take a long time. Builder ministers who want to try should figure on a commitment of at least seven to ten years.

DELIVERING THE GOODS

Anthony B. Robinson offers a helpful perspective on the challenge to offer transformational experiences facing mainline Protestants. He writes as a minister in the United Church of Christ and explains how the mainline church bodies could function for decades with "assuming the goods." Up through the 1960s these establishment churches could take for granted a civic faith and American Christendom by which Protestants understood and identified with the basics of Christian faith. They knew basic Bible stories and teaching. Special training or formation was not necessary. Being a Christian tended to take on the lowest-common-denominator meaning of being a decent person and a good citizen.

But now in our increasingly pluralistic society many have discovered they can be a good and decent person without Christian trimmings. In contrast to "assuming the goods," according to Anthony Robinson, churches today need to actually "deliver the goods," specifically in the areas of worship, teaching, and community.[14]

Lutheranism historically was not part of the American Protestant establishment. Theirs were communities of immigrants, and they looked on from the sidelines. In their ethnic associations, Lutherans were especially able to "assume the goods." A major part of Lutheran church history in the last half of the twentieth century revolved around efforts to become more "mainline." In the process of going mainline, they could easily carry their assumptions of preexisting church community into the arena of civic faith. They could continue the habit of mostly talking about or symbolizing the spiritual goods of transformed lives. But that era is now ending.

The present challenge is to learn, especially from Evangelicals, how to stay focused on providing and supporting congregational experiences that seem especially blessed by the Holy Spirit's use to touch and change lives. We are in times when actually delivering the spiritual goods in a congregation is essential to continued vitality.

QUESTIONS FOR DISCUSSION

1. What is your perspective on "religious experience" as discussed at the beginning of this chapter?

2. Would you agree with the survey observation that about one out of two Lutherans report having a "deep sense of peace during prayer," and feel "the strong presence of God during prayer"?

3. Can you recall any conversion stories you have heard?

4. Can you recognize an infant-baptizing handicap that Lutherans tend to have in evangelism?

5. How would you handle Henry Muhlenberg's invitation to discuss your first awakening?

6. What cautions would you have about recognizing an inner sense of communion with God that many Christians experience?

7. How have you experienced and taught the fruit of the Holy Spirit in Galatians 5:22, 23?

8. Of Paul's four images for salvation, which appeals to you the most: the courtroom, the slave market, the Old Testament sacrifice, and being friends with God?

9. How have you seen guilt used to motivate members of a congregation?

10. How can churches be assuming the spiritual goods rather than delivering the spiritual goods?

8

Adapting Church Culture

How well does a specific church culture invite and facilitate the work of the Holy Spirit in a fellowship's midst? That is the question this chapter addresses. Understanding the concept "culture" will help point to an answer.

The term *corporate culture* is used heavily in business circles these days. It can been defined as the specific collection of values and norms that is shared by people and groups in an organization and that controls the way they interact with each other and with stakeholders outside the organization.[1] This dry language takes on life when associated, for instance, with a CEO's pronouncement that the company's corporate culture needs to be changed to make it more responsive more rapidly to changes in their market. This in turn means staffing patterns and relationships will be streamlined, often combined with downsizing. The CEO doesn't just wake up one morning and think, We need to change our culture. It is usually in response to the lower costs of more competitors, or the need to design and produce new high-tech applications faster, or the necessity of making big investment decisions in less time. The corporation has to become better at satisfying the changing needs of customers who are in turn also responding to turbulence in their markets. Small, new companies often have a better culture for innovation than big ones that still have a culture of slow, ponderous decision structures left over from previous decades of more settled economic conditions.

Culture means the customary beliefs, social forms, and material traits of any social grouping—a family, a business, an ethnic group, a social group, a nation. A culture is made up of many customs and practices. A congregation has a culture, as does a church body. In fact, *culture* fits very well with churches. Liturgical specialists like to talk about the "cultus" as a religion's central ritual of adoration. Forms of worship epitomize cultural expressions of church life.

LUTHERAN CHURCH CUSTOMS

What does traditional Lutheran church culture look like? Janet Letnes Martin and Suzann Nelson give us a sampling in their 1997 reminiscence *Growing Up Lutheran: What Does This Mean?*[2] Somewhat tongue in cheek, they recall what they experienced through their childhood and youth. They seem about my age, so I can readily identify with their recollections. One was Norwegian Lutheran, the other German Missouri Synod Lutheran. It is amazing how similar Minnesota Lutheran culture was to Ohio Lutheran culture.

The starting point for growing up Lutheran was to be baptized as an infant. For this, the custom was and in many places still is to have two sponsors, also called godparents, a term seldom heard anymore. That used to be a much more serious responsibility, reflecting their obligation to raise the child in case the parents died—an outcome more likely at that time than today. The custom in the nineteenth century, according to my mother, was to give the first name of the sponsor as the middle name of the child; two sponsors meant two middle names, like Carl Ferdinand Wilhelm Walther. Boys had two men sponsors, girls two women. But that custom was in decline already in the early twentieth century.

Little Lutherans then went on the Cradle Roll, followed by enrollment in Sunday School (which was only for children, not adults), the high point of which was the annual year-end Sunday School Picnic. The fourth "rite of passage," according to the authors, was Vacation Bible School.

It is interesting to note how time-bound these practices of the 1950s were. Few Lutheran churches had a Sunday School in the nineteenth century. This custom came as part of a much broader nationwide Protestant Sunday School movement in the late 1800s. It was vigorously opposed by many Lutheran pastors, whose loyalty was to the weekday parochial school. In the nineteenth and early twentieth centuries, most Missouri Synod Lutheran congregations felt that to be faithful, they needed to have an elementary school, a main purpose of which was to teach their children German language and customs. Hostilities generated by the First World War against Germany put an end to that version of Lutheran culture in America. When I tried to track down past generations of the Luecke family and my mother's Luebchow family, I found that all family records from before 1918 were simply gone. That is when the German pronunciation of Lücke became the English Lūkey. It was not wise to remain German in the villages of Illinois farmland.

Vacation Bible Schools started appearing after the Second World War, and quickly became the fashion across denominations. That this custom persists indicates it is still filling a purpose. But the custom of using only denominationally generated programs is in question, as other publishers produce materials and crafts with greater appeal to those volunteers who step forward now to lead a program. A cultural breakthrough with both the Sunday School and the Vacation Bible School movements was that ordinary laypeople (mostly women) could teach Biblical truths—as long as it was to children.

The major rite of passage, of course, was confirmation at the end of elementary school. This involved memorizing Luther's Small Catechism and culminated in the dreaded Public Questioning of confirmands on Palm Sunday before the whole congregation, followed by first communion at Easter. The custom in many families was to give the successful confirmand a new Bible and a watch.

Customs do change. Many congregations now confirm on Pentecost or Reformation Day, and they use new curricula that are more student oriented. In the age of cell phones, wristwatches are becoming obsolete.

The "old-fashioned" custom of confirmation stands as perhaps the ultimate testimony to the strong sense of community and loyalty that existed in most Lutheran congregations until recent decades. Many still follow those customs, although the numbers of children involved are usually much smaller. The children had to be forced to attend. Their parents insisted on it. Many pastors brought little enthusiasm to the task of teaching junior high kids; I have heard more than one rejoice that retirement brought an end to that duty. I suspect many did not do this "duty" well. Can anyone make the case today that the older, intimidating and often joyless traditions of confirmation instruction are still the very best preparation for an adult life of discipleship? Did the results support that view?

I join Martin and Nelson with fond memories of youthful involvement in Walther League and Luther League. Our Walther League had our monthly meetings in a room with a stained-glass panel of the Walther League symbol. I became zone president and enjoyed working with a dozen other church leagues. The Walther League, of course, disappeared already in the 1960s.

ADAPTING CUSTOMS TO CHANGED CIRCUMSTANCES

Lutherans are not the only church culture that needs to update its customs for confirming children in their faith. Noting the steep decline in Catholic Mass attendance, four sociologists recently observed that younger Catholics have to be persuaded—rather than ordered—to attend Mass. Their findings in *American Catholics Today: New Realities of Their Faith and Church* include the observations that for youth, the church is now only one of many possible means to help them meet their own needs.[3] Religion is a choice, a cafeteria choice. These researchers conclude that to reach younger generations, the Catholic Church will have to adapt not its core doctrine, but its approach.

Consider yet another youth-oriented culture that has had to change its ways in order to achieve its basic purposes. This is the United States Army, which has been at war in Iraq for seven years as of this writing. Brian Mockenhaupt describes "The Army We Have."[4] For an ongoing force of 512,000, the Army has to recruit and train 80,000 new soldiers a year. With the draft for Vietnam, the Army had a "soft" recruitment environment; they could get through the draft all the soldiers they wanted. In the present absence of a way to force young people to serve, the Army's task of recruiting and training new soldiers has become much more difficult. They now have a "hard" environment. Service in the military has to be made attractive enough to entice young men and women to volunteer. Those who qualify come with high personal expectations for how they will be treated, because they have many competing ways to invest their time and energy.

According to Mockenhaupt, "the Army has shifted the culture of basic training away from the demeaning treatment and harsh indoctrination that have always characterized standing armies. Drill sergeants are supposed to act more as coaches and mentors than as feared disciplinarians. They yell less; swearing and abusive language is no longer tolerated." Also, "The less-threatening and more-respectful environment helps recruit new soldiers and lowers the attrition rate."

Overall the Army has shifted to a kinder and gentler approach. The beat-upon Beetle Bailey of comic strip fame is long gone from today's Army.

Another measure of the hard environment is that officers now are evaluated on the retention rate for those serving under them, something not of much importance in drafted armies.

The Army had it much easier when they had the option of depending on law and even imprisonment to provide as many recruits as they wanted. One can speculate whether traditional congregations with strong loyalty of parents had what amounted to a draft, that provided recruits for confirmation regardless of what these junior high children thought about this part of their life.

Whether we in the church like it or not, the environment for ministry among teens and young adults has hardened considerably, as it has for other institutions. This is especially true for infant-baptizing church bodies that counted on families to raise up their children to be the congregation of the next generation. Churches have to work much harder now to even have a next generation.

CHURCH CULTURE

In broadest terms, a Christian church's customs and culture develop around how these believers present and receive truths of the Bible, how they do Baptism and the Lord's Supper, how they pray, what they sing and how they make music, the ways they raise their children and take in new participants, the social activities they engage in.

We can speak about the ways a church's culture hosts the Holy Spirit. Some expect the Spirit to come quickly and dramatically, raising strong emotions. Others expect little of the Spirit beyond nudging hearts when the Word of God is presented; they may seldom pray that God the Father release more of his Spirit in their midst. Relying on good things to come from the Word, Lutherans typically have very low expectations of the Spirit's noticeable movement.

Churches may share the same beliefs but express them a little differently from congregation to congregation. A church body's culture changes from decade to decade, and of course from century to century. Using a new language forces many cultural changes. There are those in any ethnic immigrant group who resist adopting the dominant language of their new country because they fear their culture will change. Some congregations in The Lutheran Church—Missouri Synod still worshipped and transacted their business in German well into the 1950s.[5] Those Germans were right. Lutheran culture did indeed change. One way that they would never have anticipated is the more formal and extensive worship liturgies that appeared in the new English hymnals.[6]

Those churches whose framework for church life is liturgy talk about the Christian church as having a distinctive culture. Liturgical scholar Thomas Schattauer proposes that such a culture should form a wall separating through word, action, and sense the churchly life from all that is wrong with everyday life. This calls for worship with "ritual and symbolic density, that recovers 'dramatic density.' "[7] And indeed many congregations do practice symbolic and dramatic density with their specialized vocabulary, their heavy usage of visual symbols all around the sanctuary and their celebration of saint days throughout the major parts of the church year. All this, of course, assumes very advanced understanding of so much detail. What would the building of dense walls of churchly culture say about the purpose of a church that pursues such a vision? Might it be that offering mature Christians a refuge from the world seems to be a greater concern than mission into it?

Shepherd pastors do well in a church culture that stays mostly the same over the years. In fact, negotiating this culture, with its ways of communicating God's Word and of worshipping, may well be the pastor's central professional competence. Purposely changing that culture to make it more accessible to those not yet there understandably has little appeal.

Builder ministers accept change for mission purposes. Change is inherent in the building process. They are willing, for instance, to test innovations in worship practices and thus worship culture in order to see and evaluate the results.

TRY DIFFERENT TECHNIQUES

Consider church culture in terms of techniques. A technique is a set of detailed steps or movements taken toward accomplishing a desired outcome. Carpenters have techniques and the appropriate tools for hanging a door with its moldings. Cooks have techniques for preparing a turkey. Business offices have a technique for processing orders with minimal confusion. Physicians follow specified steps to diagnose an illness and established procedures for treating it; these techniques are also called a protocol. A set of techniques makes up a technology—a well-established way to produce something effectively and efficiently. High tech means advanced reliance on computer processing.

Do churches follow techniques for accomplishing their work? Certainly. There are techniques for preaching—lectionary, topical or expository. So are there many techniques for praying—done only by the pastor, done alone in private, shared in groups, written formally, in response to solicited requests. Contemporary worship teams can pick songs based on the top 40 they hear on Christian radio or by the most popular in church usage as determined by CCLI licensing. All the tools in the chapter 4 discussion of the builder's toolbox—communicating the Word well, keeping Sacraments in balance with Word, planning worship that is engaging, confessing sins, sharing prayer, pursuing relationships for comfort and encouragement, hearing spiritual experiences of others, seeing the Spirit at work in other places—consist of techniques for shaping church life.

Usual techniques make up customs, which in turn express a culture. All that can be considered as tradition. Changing a whole church culture can be an overwhelming undertaking for a minister. It is likely to be resisted by those who like their customs just as they are. But changing a specific technique for specified purposes, such as to build fellowship through new ways to share prayer, is easier to understand and accept—and to do. New techniques that work better add up to a more fruitful congregation.

In chapter 5 I observed that you cannot expect much forward movement of a congregation by doing the same old things the same old ways with the same people. Changing some techniques can make a difference.

You cannot expect people to try a new way of doing something just by hearing it described, especially when it comes with a label like more Catholic, more Evangelical, or contemporary. It has to be modeled. If the minister or members of a congregation cannot model it, pray that God send someone who can. In the church plant I did, several families from Pentecostal backgrounds showed us new ways to pray—in the service and in special gatherings. They came to share a new fellowship, and I encouraged them to express prayers in the service and to start a prayer group. Some of them are in the prayer group pictured on the cover of my book, *Talking with God.*[8] They remained uncomfortable with infant baptizing, and they eventually left for yet another fellowship new to them. I thanked God for this temporary blessing.

Remember the concept of liminality from the end of chapter 4 on tools? *Liminality* means threshold. When Christians are at the edge of old experience and starting to perceive new experiences, they are more open to the Holy Spirit's efforts to transform their priorities and commitments. Liminal techniques serve to put them on the threshold of new perceptions.

Mission experiences can do that. So can sending leaders to conferences. I took a group of seven from Royal Redeemer to a leadership weekend at a well-known Lutheran church.[9] It was transformational for our prayer ministry. The conference ended with the four pastors each praying for about a dozen participants. At the airport on the way home, we arrived at a threshold for new understanding of the Holy Spirit while comparing reports of what the pastor had prayed for each of us individually. For five in the group, he had raised up things about each that he would have had no human way of knowing. Later, when I talked about this with the senior pastor, he commented, "Yes, the Spirit was heavy on us that morning." Experiencing the possibilities from fervent prayer gave new energy to our prayer efforts.

A WELCOME CHANGE IN LUTHERAN CULTURE

Most ministers and church leaders would agree today that having more members ready and able to give personal witness to their faith would be a positive change in Lutheran church culture.

Consider some teaching techniques that may have contributed to the passivity behind this reluctance. Classic Lutheran teaching, as well as preaching, was highly lecture oriented. The teacher/pastor would describe a teaching and support it with Scripture passages. Students listened and tried to remember. A basic lesson being taught was that there is a right way to say something and, by implication, everything else is wrong. That applies to worship, too. Failure to have the right answer when called upon in a class often brought punishment, like a rap on the knuckles with a ruler. I personally remember this happening when I was in the first grade of the school in our Lutheran church. The lesson being learned is that with religious things, saying nothing is better than running the risk of getting it wrong. Those teachers learned this approach from their teachers in a German culture. We can be thankful teachers educated in English-language accredited colleges learned better, more positive ways to motivate students.

Maybe such passivity and avoidance helps account for the consistent outcome of surveys done by Lutheran insurance companies that. even in recent decades. half of Lutheran respondents agree they will be saved by the good life they lead. This does not at all agree with the Gospel of grace they were taught, but it might be consistent with the church life they experienced. Perhaps these respondents assumed that Lutherans have all the right answers; they are working hard to be good Lutherans; therefore they will be saved by that good life. Might they have never personalized the meaning of those answers? Confessing Christ even passively will bring salvation. But passive Lutherans will probably not be good witnesses in words of their own.

Techniques for teaching in Lutheran churches and schools have changed, of course. Much more emphasis is placed on getting children active doing, writing and saying things. So what are some techniques that can help adults become more comfortable sharing their faith? First, teach beyond lectures on head knowledge and discussions that get the facts right. Teach also by inviting participants to share their experiences and feelings, as discussed in the previous chapter. Help them identify and tell their personal spiritual journeys, with highlights of their times of discovering new dimensions of their faith in God. Demonstrate how others tell their story. Encourage testimonies in classes. Testimonies in a church service can be unwieldy and time-consuming, but current technology makes the recording and time-conscious editing of stories within a congregation feasible. One-minute video accounts of personal witnessing events are available through the Mission Services department of The Lutheran Church—Missouri Synod.

One of the easiest ways to get passive Lutherans to talk about their faith is by engaging them in shared prayer—prayer that has them expressing their prayer relationships with God out loud with others. Small groups can model such expressions and provide support that builds confidence to try.

Of course it is important to keep the Biblical facts straight. But remember that Biblical faith comes in two forms: head knowledge of Biblical teachings, plus heart knowledge of encounters with God.

FAITHFUL TO WHAT?

One central issue in churches is whether or not a given change in a church's cultural expression, like worship, means that the core doctrinal beliefs have been changed. The question should always be asked.

It is easy, though, to confuse core beliefs with the cultural means of expressing them. Customary ways of communicating and doing things form the basics of a culture.

In many ways, the fast-moving, high-tech American culture of today is light years away from Paul's time of slow communication without printing presses and of travel on foot. But in other ways, as noted in chapter 1, the current urban and increasingly hostile dominant culture we face now is getting more like what Paul faced. Cultures are always in transition—sometimes slowly, over centuries in the Middle Ages, but never as swiftly as now, with our advertising-driven media saturation and personalized Internet searches and postings. For those of us over thirty years old with children in school, it is sobering to realize that they live in a world very different from our own experience of growing up.

Changed cultures are what make interpreting the Bible so challenging. The first task is necessarily to determine what the inspired writer, Paul, for instance, meant for the readers to understand at that time. Consider his expectation in 1 Corinthians 11 that women should have long hair and pray with their heads covered. He was encouraging respectful compliance with role expectations of that culture, especially as seen in Corinth, a city noted for unconstrained sexual behavior. Figuring out the meaning then and there is the exegetical task. Next comes recognition of the changes in language and cultures over the millennia and how they separate that culture from the one we are in here and now. Our task is to interpret that basic meaning into equivalent terms and practices now. Few today would interpret short hair on women as a sign of disrespect, and the rarity of seeing women with hats in worship now suggests that such head covering no longer has symbolic value. The condition of the heart is more important than the dress. For those who like specialized vocabulary, interpreting the "then and there" into its equivalent "here and now" is called the hermeneutical challenge.

Church bodies which have formative confessions from Reformation times face the same challenge of interpreting those intentions into language and practices of today. Those were days when what the ruler believed was what the people believed; that is, they were state churches where individuals had no choice. Reformation churches survived their early years, not because their teachings were popular—which they were—but because a small alliance of princes were able to offer protection. The Smalcald League crumbled when a few key leaders changed sides, and the league lost independence from the Emperor when they were defeated in battle in 1547. When Duke Maurice of Saxony switched back to the League, these Lutherans forced the Emperor to accept the Religious Peace of Augsburg in 1555. That is why and how the formative Augsburg Confession of 1530 remained in widespread usage through the following centuries.

Dealing with the variance of practices in those eight interim years led, by the way, to the confessional principle in the Formula of Concord of 1580 that the community of God in every place and at every time has the authority to change, to reduce, and/or to increase ceremonies according to its circumstances.[10] "Ceremonies" was their word for what we now call "liturgy," itself a word not used in the Lutheran Confessions except in one footnote. That politically derived mandate for freedom in matters of public worship has become important again in the worship struggles of today.

Those protective centuries of state churches are long gone in America today. Church bodies survive now by how well they are able to meet the spiritual needs of people in the current culture.

Tradition is very important in any church. Being faithful to a church body's traditions has much to say for it. Yet one needs to ask whether faithfulness to church tradition is the faithfulness the apostle Paul would recognize and encourage. The version of life in Christ that he led did break a lot of traditions among Jewish followers of the Messiah. Sharp dispute with those who insisted on tradition led the church in Antioch to send Paul and Barnabas "to go to Jerusalem to see the apostles and elders about this question." That background and the high-level meeting that resulted are described in Acts 15:1–29. The issue was what Jewish traditions could and what could not change when Gentiles became followers of Christ.

Paul accepted the council's conclusion—which seemed good to the Holy Spirit as well as to them—that they should not burden Gentiles with Jewish customs but still respect Jewish believers. Gentiles need not be circumcised, but they should observe kosher laws when they meet together to eat with Jewish Christians. Such high-level meetings to work out the path of faithful practices make a lot of sense for church bodies today that take their traditions seriously.

Because traditions do change, as some get lost and others added, one needs to ask which version of tradition should be faithfully followed—sixteenth century German, eighteenth century Norwegian, the mid-1800s, or the 1910s, or the 1950s in America? Which is the right version of tradition to keep for posterity? One thinks of Hasidic Jews that froze their heritage of Jewish beliefs and practices into the forms and distinctive clothing—black frock coat and black wide-brimmed hat—of mid-nineteenth century Poland. Is that what tradition-oriented but mission-minded Protestant churches should try to emulate today?

In a review of a book I wrote,[11] Richard John Neuhaus criticized efforts to reduce a communication gap with those the church is trying to reach. I had suggested Lutherans could learn how better to communicate the Gospel, specifically, how to build an audience and to make personal faith statements. He claimed that "Christianity is a distinctive worldview, with a distinctive vocabulary, distinctive moral sensibilities, and a distinctive way of being in the world. It is . . . a cultural-linguistic tradition. One must be initiated into it, one must make a decision about it, one must cross the gap into another world."[12]

Well said for one widespread understanding of church tradition. But how different this is from seeing Christianity as all about relationships—redeemed relationships with Jesus Christ and changed relationships with each other. The world to cross over into is the one the Holy Spirit opens in the everyday life of those who hear Christ's call to follow him. Initiation should be into a relationship, not just a culture. Culture is only a servant for God's action.

The faithfulness to be recommended is to the heritage of Scriptures and the church body's confessions. This should not be confused with faithfulness to an ever-changing tradition.

QUESTIONS FOR DISCUSSION

1. Have you heard about any corporations trying to change their cultures?

2. What are aspects of your church's culture that stand out for you?

3. Does any one custom of Lutheran church culture stand out as your favorite?

4. How well does your congregation's church culture host the Holy Spirit's work among them?

5. Identify four techniques of prayer that you and your congregation use. Do you know of other techniques you would like to try?

6. What, if any, changes in Lutheran church culture would you like to bring about?

7. What does being faithful in ministry mean to you?

PART IV: PROCESSES

9

Organizing to Build Up the Fellowship

The assignment given to church leaders by the apostle Paul in his writing to the Ephesians was, "Prepare God's people for works of service, so that the body of Christ may be built up" (4:12). In chapter 4 I offered the interpretation, "Get fellow members aligned for ministries that build up the body of Christ!"

As developed in chapter 4, New Testament usage of the word translated in the NIV as "prepare" ("equip" in the RSV translation) carried the meaning to be restored to a relationship, fitted together, brought into alignment with a standard. Matthew uses this Greek word to describe what James and John were doing when Jesus called them to follow—they were "mending" their nets (Matthew 4:21). They were getting the cords restored to the intended pattern of small gaps that fish could not slip through. They got the cords realigned.

Align is a relationship term. Today we get automobile wheels aligned so that all four are going in precisely the same direction. In word processing, lines are aligned to start the same distance from the left edge of the paper.

How do you align the members of a church to do a better job of building up its fellowship? More precisely, how do you get them in the right relationships to each other and to God and also to get them in line with the same mission of a congregation?

You begin, of course, with preaching and teaching the Gospel of God's relationship with his people.

In the horizontal relationships of God's people with each other in his church, it is helpful to recognize the difference between the congregation as fellowship and the congregation as a formal organization.

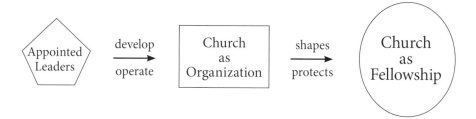

ORGANIZATION AND FELLOWSHIP

In the chart above, the big circle on the right represents all the possible relationships going on in a specific congregation—the pattern of interactions members have with each other within the fellowship as well as beyond, plus their personal relationships with Christ as the head of the church. In a healthy fellowship, these relationships will be many and strong. They include several members getting together for coffee and Christian consolation, also a member witnessing at work, a conversation going on during the coffee hour on Sunday, a member family doing devotions at home, an informal group of men, some of which are members, eating breakfast together once a week, and a member tutoring kids downtown on his way home from work on Tuesdays. In short, the informal fellowship is all the interactions going on in addition to those scheduled by the church.

The church as organization focuses on just some of those patterns of relationships, the ones prescribed in constitutions and bylaws as additions to the informal structure of the basic fellowship. Such formal structure of intended relationships is a tool used to shape and protect the reality of the more extensive informal relationships among the members.

Appointed leaders develop and guide the tool of formal organization so that the broader fellowship stays healthy. Such leadership chooses which patterns of relationships will be emphasized and how this will be done. The job of these leaders is to develop and operate the church as an organization so it can shape and protect the church as a fellowship.

This tool of formal organization can solve some problems. But often it can do little to change other conditions. If a fellowship is weak and declining, its organization should be considering what changes to make to restore health. Just doing more of the same is probably not going to accomplish a significant change in health.

HISTORICAL CHANGES IN CHURCH ORGANIZATION

Historically, a congregation's formal organization in the nineteenth century was typically a lot smaller than one finds today: a few trustees to take care of money and property, a few elders to address people problems, and a pastor to carry out the ministry of Word and Sacraments. This was possible because of a high overlap between church community (the fellowship) and the broader social community, which overlapped the geographic community. Relationships were many and strong.

By the 1960s and 70s, many church fellowships were weakening because the overlap was decreasing. Members moved farther away and found new and different social networks to pursue their interests. The then-prevailing theory was that you got people "involved" in the congregation by putting them on committees. Administrative leaders fashioned organizational solutions by establishing a half dozen or many more committees and boards to do specific tasks, writing out expectations, setting meeting schedules, and getting fifty to a hundred members assigned annually to these "boxes" of responsibility. This was the committee structure of the 60s and 70s.

At least three problems emerged. The most obvious was getting people to serve enthusiastically in the specified roles, especially when, as often happened, they were told they would not have to do much. Such involvement assumed a lot of loyalty. The second was the confusion and frustration resulting from not knowing who was actually doing what, especially when many of the committees were really not functioning. The third was increasing the guilt of members who accepted responsibilities they could not find time for, often driving them further away from the fellowship.

Today the formal organization of vibrant congregations is probably smaller and simpler than it was in the 1980s. They are likely to have a small board of directors to take care of governance issues and a separate ministry structure to guide and support members doing various ministries. Rather than fitting members into predetermined organizational boxes whether or not they have much interest, administrative leaders are becoming more adept at fitting organizational support around those members who bring passion and commitment to specific ministry areas.

ORGANIZING VOLUNTEERS OR MINISTERS?

One approach to aligning workers for ministry in a congregation is to borrow from the experience of organizations that manage many volunteers. Think of the Red Cross with its one million volunteers. Their manuals stress the importance of being very clear about what the volunteer is expected to do, providing necessary training, supervising carefully, and giving plenty of encouragement. A classic church version of this model was offered thirty years ago by Douglas W. Johnson in the *Care and Feeding of Volunteers*.[1] A later version is *Empowering Lay Volunteers*.[2] Writing for church leaders, Johnson's topics include: Identifying and Recruiting Volunteers, Giving Assignments, Training, Helping Volunteers Plan, and Running Meetings. Both Johnson and the Red Cross do variations on the basic functions taught for any kind of management: planning, organizing, staffing, operating, and evaluating.

There are two limits to this approach. One is that it takes a lot of paid staff to make it work. The Red Cross is one of the most effective fund-raising organizations in the country and can afford such staffing. For many congregations, finding the funds to hire any staff beyond the minister is one of the basic limitations they live with.

The second limitation comes through the assumption that, with church volunteers, no greater motivation is involved than that of a volunteer in any secular organization. In many churches this may well be true. But Christian congregations that understand and cultivate their distinctive nature should anticipate more. Somewhere the Holy Spirit needs to be figured into the mix.

The apostle Paul knew what to look for. In 1 Corinthians 12 and Romans 12, he anticipated that the Holy Spirit would provide special motivation by which each member of the fellowship could and would contribute something special to the common good. This was the starting assumption. The leaders just needed to figure out who had what gifting and how to get them into action. Paul would not have talked about volunteers. He regarded everybody as a minister—ready to move beyond passive involvement to active service to others.

THE CHURCH IS A SPIRITUAL COMMUNITY

The question of motivation calls for clear understanding of the basic nature of a Christian congregation. Chapter 6 explained different models of the church as presented by Avery Dulles. One is the church as *institution*, which is the Roman Catholic model, and is far from recognizing everyone as a minister and does not talk much about relying upon the Holy Spirit. The church as *servant* sees the congregation's purpose as serving social needs beyond itself, and would be comfortable talking about volunteers much like the Red Cross does. Douglas Johnson writes for the audience of liberal United Methodist churches. A third model sees a church as *herald* with the distinctive purpose of bringing Christ to those who do not know him. Many Evangelical churches have such a high priority, but in the process lose focus on the other basic functions, like worship and service.

The model that best fits orthodox Reformation theology is the church as spiritual communion.[3] The best description is the formation of the Christian church in Jerusalem on Pentecost, the day of the Holy Spirit, in Acts 2. That first congregation became a fellowship that served one another (2:45), and one of the reasons the early churches grew so fast is their reputation for loving one another. Those churches of new and enthusiastic followers of Christ were miles beyond being just a social fellowship or service organization, of which there were many in Roman culture.

FORMAL ORGANIZATION AND THE HOLY SPIRIT

In the mid-1980s I taught a course at Fuller Theological Seminary on the Holy Spirit in Church Organization. For me it was part of the same quest I pursue now: How do you get more of the Holy Spirit's presence and energy through formal organization of a church? To my surprise, all of the dozen students came from Pentecostal and charismatic backgrounds. They were hoping to bring more order and predictability into the spiritual passions they knew so well. Students from mainstream long-established church bodies apparently did not find it compelling to learn how the Holy Spirit works. By now, after twenty more years of decline, leaders of old-line churches should be getting more curious.

The two—the unpredictable Holy Spirit and the highly valued predictability of customs and church organization—will always be in tension. The one does not follow human job descriptions very well but works according to God's plan. The other likes order, predictability and control. Left to itself, the human process of organizing and managing is likely to squeeze the unpredictable Spirit out of consideration.

Better organization is probably not the key to turning around withering congregations or withering church bodies—unless the organization stays open to the ways of the Holy Spirit and stops siphoning off members' energy in unproductive ways.

The basic problem of withering churches is more likely spiritual than organizational. Most churches today face a loss of "energy"—an all-purpose word to describe commitment, time, and resources once given willingly by members for the good of the Christian congregation. The best way to generate new energy is to cultivate the soil of church life and culture in ways that give more opportunities for the Spirit to work on the hearts of members. Better organization can be a help by featuring, for instance, prayer, Bible study and the mutual conversation and consolation of the brethren in small groups. Organization can be a hindrance if it absorbs too much leadership time in formalities of structure, like monthly committee meetings. Actually *doing* ministry is better than just *talking* about ministry.

BETTER ORGANIZATION

To understand church organization better, recognize that any continuing cluster of relationships, including a church, inherently has a *structure*, that is, a pattern to how the parts fit together. A family has a pattern for how father, mother, older child, and younger child interact with each other. A congregation has a pattern for how members interact; for instance, who leads and who follows when worshiping together, who keeps track of the money, who steps forward to encourage others, who (if anybody) greets visitors. A social psychologist could look at a congregation of a hundred members and easily find thousands of relationships that follow a pattern as they carry on life together over a month or a year. Some of those relationships would include those listed in this chapter's earlier discussion of informal fellowship: conversations over coffee, telephone calls of consolation, witness at work, home family devotions, regular breakfast and lunches together, time spent in community social services. With such observation a sociologist could map a structure of relationships that might be quite complicated. Most of this would be *informal* structure.

When we talk about organization today, we are usually talking about *formal* structure—patterns that are specified ahead of time, often in writing. *Formal organization* is the world of job descriptions, reporting relationships, monthly meetings, deadlines, and financial reports. Formal organization is a tool to accomplish intended purposes. This formal organizational structure usually develops to solve problems the leaders think are the most important.

Why do people conform to predictable patterns of relationships, especially formally stated relationships? One of the earliest sociologists, Max Weber, highlighted three basic reasons. The first is attraction to a *charismatic leader* who gives direction. Jesus was charismatic in the sense of being attractive; his followers were so impressed they tried hard to do what he told them. The second is by force of *tradition*, according to which some established customary patterns of relationships are simply replicated from year to year; the people may change, but the patterns stay the same. The third explanation to why people conform is that the intended pattern has been *rationally established*; that is, reasoning and logic about cause and effect have been used to determine that a certain Pattern A is better than a Pattern B. For instance, having most policy decisions of a congregation made by a small representative board of directors (A) is better than making decisions by submitting all planned changes to a vote of all members (B).

The world moved slowly enough into much of the twentieth century that patterns of church life could be carried forward by tradition. And tradition worked well. The only compelling reason to move beyond replicating what was done in the past by tradition is that those patterns are no longer working as they should, or at least as well as they used to. The ever-present question is why. The answers today usually have to do with the loss of the strong sense of community and loyalty a congregation probably had in the past.

A major problem for church bodies that honor their long traditions is how to shift from patterns carried on by tradition to patterns established by rational development of new formal structures. This is happening in many congregations with something called Policy-Based Governance. Instead of having decisions made by a Voters' Assembly or a large council, decisions on governance—for example, establishing a budget or adding a staff position—are assigned to a small board of directors. Then those doing and especially leading specific ministries—for example, assimilation or publicity—establish whatever structure makes sense to them to do their ministry effectively, communicating as efficiently as possible, usually now by e-mail. Most adults today are very time-conscious and are increasingly sensitive to not having their time wasted.

NATURAL CHURCH DEVELOPMENT

Structure for planning the formal organization of a congregation is offered by German theologian and church growth expert Christian A. Schwarz. He calls his approach Natural Church Development (NCD). It presents a guide to eight essential qualities of healthy churches. His method and materials are used by many consultants and staff of denominations to help declining congregations assess needs and develop strategies.

The traditional patterns for a church's formal organization revolve around functions focusing on input, like plans for worship, for education of children adults, for service and evangelism. In contrast, Christian Schwarz starts with basic outcomes. They are:

Passionate spirituality	Functional structures
Inspiring worship service	Holistic small groups
Gift-oriented ministry	Need-oriented evangelism
Empowering leadership	Loving relationships

These quality characteristics emerged through analysis of questionnaire research on over one thousand different churches on six continents, "large and small, growing and declining, persecuted and state-subsidized, charismatic and noncharismatic, prominent model and entirely unknown church." The purpose was to decide "which of the modern 'principles of success' are universally applicable and which are simply 'myths.'"[4] Most of the Church Growth efforts in the 1980s used the single criterion of numeric growth or decline in attendance to asses a congregation. Resistance rightfully claimed that growth in quality is also significant. Such quality, like loving relationships, is built into the Natural Church Growth data. The German perspective is helpful just in terms of its vocabulary. Church Growth is *Gemeinde Aufbau*, which literally means "fellowship up building." This understanding is closer to the concept that Paul expressed in Greek.

In the Schwarz approach, congregations are assessed by member and leader responses to a questionnaire, analysis of which produces a score for each quality characteristic, and an overall score based on the eight. The median score is set at 50. In NCD research, congregations with a combined quality score of 65 or over almost always (99.4%) report quantitative growth. Schwarz asserts, "Whenever I visit churches where the '65 hypothesis' holds true, I always have a strong pervading sense of the presence of the Holy Spirit."[5]

A congregation I know of had a combined NCD score of 27, which is nigh unto death. Indeed, a few years later it merged with another. The resulting merged church is showing new energy. The merger may turn out to be an igniter event for new congregational health.

The church I serve had a score of 59 ten years ago. This is good, but not near 65. The highest qualities were empowering leadership and functional structures. But the score on the quality of our wholistic group life was quite low. We have yet to make significant progress on that *quality*. Our *quantitative* growth has stopped. Consultants observe that churches frequently get stuck in their growth at an average attendance of 1,000. Increasing the number and kind of relationships between members, especially new ones, is part of the key to continued growth.

The last of the eight quality characteristics listed above is "loving relationships." In 1986, Win and Charles Arn published the results of survey studies they did that led to a Love/Care Quotient. They sought responses from members of various churches to such questions as frequency of use of such phrases as "I love you," and "How loving is your church to each other and to visitors?" They had enough responses from congregations of a number of church bodies so that they could produce a Love/Care Quotient by denominations.

The most loving turned out to be Southern Baptists, Church of God and some other Evangelical church bodies. At the bottom of the list were The Lutheran Church—Missouri Synod and Christian Reformed.

Would you expect loving and sharing churches to grow numerically better than those with a low L/CQ? The only score lower than that for the LCMS was for Christian Reformed churches, which form another denomination that has strong ethnic roots, in their case Dutch.[6]

SOME INSIGHTS ABOUT QUALITY

Here are some specific insights from Christian Schwarz's research as reported in his book *Natural Church Development.* I have rearranged the order of qualities to put the more evident issues of spirituality at the beginning.

Passionate Spirituality

The nature of this quality characteristic becomes evident by examining the prayer life of the Christians surveyed. . . . Whether prayer is viewed (by the individual) as an "inspiring experience" or not has a significant relationship to the quality and quantity of the church. Similar results were found with respect to personal use of the Bible and other factors affecting personal spirituality.

"Pure doctrine" alone does not induce growth. A church, regardless of how orthodox its dogma and view of Scripture, can hardly expect to experience growth, as long as its members do not learn to live their faith with contagious enthusiasm and to share it with others.

Inspiring worship service

Services may target Christians or non-Christians, their style may be liturgical or free, their language may be "churchy" or "secular"—it makes no difference for church growth.

"Inspiring" is to be understood in the literal sense of *inspiratio* and means an inspiredness which comes from the Spirit of God. Whenever the Holy Spirit is truly at work (and His presence is not merely presumed), He will have a concrete effect upon the way a worship service is conducted, including the entire atmosphere of a gathering. People attending truly "inspired" services typically indicate that "going to church is fun."

(An objection might be that Christians) go to church to fulfill their Christian duty. These people do not attend church because it is a joyous and inspiring experience, but to do the pastor or God a favor. . . . When worship is inspiring, it draws people to the services "all by itself."

Gift-oriented Ministry

None of the eight quality characteristics showed nearly as much influence on both personal and church life as "gift-oriented ministry." This is why it doesn't surprise me at all that the practical tools we have developed on this quality characteristic have had by far the best reception of all our church growth materials.

The discovery and use of spiritual gifts is the only way to live out the Reformation watchword of the "priesthood of all believers."

Empowering Leadership

Leaders of growing churches concentrate on empowering other Christians for ministry. They do not use lay workers as "helpers" in attaining their own goals and fulfilling their own visions. Rather they invert the pyramid of authority so that the leader assists Christians to gain the spiritual potential God has for them.

Functional Structures

Our research confirmed for the first time an extremely negative relationship between traditionalism and both growth and quality within the church.

Holistic Small Groups

We found that there is an enormous difference, for example, between church leadership discussing "evangelism," "loving relationships," or "gift-oriented ministry" in its staff meetings, and having each Christian, integrated into a small group, go through a process in which he or she experiences the meaning of these terms practically expressed in the life of the group.

Need-oriented Evangelism

The key to church growth is for the local congregation to focus its evangelistic efforts on the questions and needs of non-Christians. This "need-oriented" approach is different from "manipulative programs" where pressure on non-Christians must compensate for the lack of need-orientation.

Challenging Christians to build new relationships with non-Christians is most certainly not a growth principle. The point is rather to use already-existing relationships as contact for evangelism.

Loving relationships

It can be demonstrated that there is a significant relationship between "laughter in the church" and that church's qualitative and numerical growth. People do not want to hear us talk about love, they want to experience how Christian love really works.

WHAT TO DO?

Once a congregation knows its quality scores on the eight characteristics, what's next? Forming eight committees is probably not going to do the job. Basically, NCD promotes focus on how to improve the weakest quality and how to rely on your stronger qualities to do that. This is not the place to go into specifics of Natural Church Development. Church Smart Resources (www.churchsmart.com) is the American base. It offers a variety of resources to help turn insights into action.

It would be great if we were back in the simpler times of the 1950s when denominational staff could develop programs by writing job descriptions, schedules and promotional material. Congregations were more alike then, and higher member loyalty brought willingness to spend the time going through the outlined steps. To the extent programs of any sort are still out there, they mostly come from those para-church organizations.

But those organizations now usually operate more like diagnostic consultants than programmers. They know there are no simple answers. Many high-visibility church leaders have stepped forward to say they have found the way. This might be true for them, each with a distinctive personality, and for their congregation at that time, place, and size. But those answers seldom translate well to congregations made up of different leaders and followers at different times, places, size and history. This truth amounts to one of the most important insights from the last twenty or so years of promoting growth and worrying about decline.

Teaching in the doctor of ministry program at Fuller Theological Seminary, I once had as a student a minister whose self-selected project was to plan a building project with the necessary fund-raising effort for his congregation. It was page after page of assignments and job descriptions. I gave it a low grade because it looked like all the many verbal boxes came out of a manual of some sort. He did not understand that the real challenge is not to write out assignments but rather to motivate members toward a specific common outcome. How to do such motivation will differ from congregation to congregation.

For purposeful transformative growth of a congregation, there is no real alternative to having a core group of church leaders—driven by spiritual commitments and eager to help others experience church life driven by the Gospel—prayerfully looking for ways to bring movement to their specific congregation at that time and place. Central to the group has to be a builder minister.

In current times, traditional shepherd assumptions are seldom associated with significant quantitative growth of a congregation. One important weakness is that the shepherd model does not focus on multiplying relationships.

PLANNING, VISION, AND POLICY

Basic to shifting from tradition to effective formal organization in a congregation is rational planning that identifies alternatives and then, through discussion, chooses one over the others.

Planning became much discussed and emphasized in the decades when churches began to look for organizational solutions to their problems. I have written and done my share. Here are three overall generalizations.

1. The better the analysis, the better the chances that a plan will fit and make a difference. I have found good outcomes with the basic business school framework of SWOT-S. Envision a group discussing and having someone write down on newsprint:

   The **S**trengths and **W**eaknesses within a specific congregation

   The **O**pportunities and **T**hreats in the environment around the congregation **S**atisfactions (outcomes) that the congregation wants to deliver

   The point for the planning group is to decide which strengths will be used to address which opportunities (or avoid which threats) to achieve which outcomes that are the highest priority. Planning is all about making choices. The downfall of much church planning is avoiding hard decisions, and such avoidance is one of the basic reasons formal planning in churches often has little impact on church life and health.

2. The written plan, even if choices have been made on paper, needs to be applied consistently to decisions made throughout the formal structure of the

church organization. Administrative consistency is hard to achieve anywhere, but especially in churches. Somebody's needs and preferences are going to go unattended. The sincere desire to continue to please everybody soon reduces a plan to a report collecting dust on a shelf. A plan, say, to re-focus financial resources away from a day-care center that never grew and can't cover its expenses, and then to use the funds for building up a small-group ministry, is obviously going to leave day-care advocates unhappy. Closing programs in a church fellowship is very hard to do.

3. The plan needs to win the assent of all who participate in the formal organization. A small planning team that does not invite the input of others is likely to yield the problems of point 2. The other standing committees usually ignore a plan they did not help shape. That behavior is hardly unique to churches.

Vision Setting has received a lot of attention in church leadership circles, especially in the last several decades. Much has been written. The best is by Aubrey Malphurs.[7]

He distinguishes between a mission statement and a vision. A mission is a brief, broad statement of intent that should reflect Biblical mandates. A vision is what the ministry will look like as it accomplishes its mission in its unique community. It is a detailed description of a brief mission statement.

Malphurs offers the following distinctions:

Mission is	Vision is
a Statement	a Snapshot
Planning	Communication
Short	Long
Informs	Inspires
Doing	Seeing
Head	Heart
Clarifies	Challenges
Taught	Caught
Verbal	Visual

As with planning, a vision can be easily written out with lots of detail on a piece of paper. The challenge is to have it caught and accepted by all members of the congregation. This takes years of consistency in describing and applying the vision. It is far from a gimmick to be tried out for a meeting or two.

There will be more on strategic planning in chapter 11.

Policy. As mentioned earlier, many churches have found improvement in their formal organization structure by distinguishing between a structure for governance and a different one for ministry. This is part of avoiding the dysfunctional structures found to be so important in Christian Schwarz's research.

The *governance* structure should take as little time from as few people as possible. It can be done with an elected board of directors meeting quarterly. Its responsibility is to look after property and to set policies for work done within the formal organization. The ministry or *administrative* structure is to guide and support the ministries done by both unpaid and paid leaders within the parameters of policy. It is for the "doers."

Policy-based governance is an approach written about and taught by John Carver.[8] It has become popular among many congregations, especially the larger ones. Carver attractively describes the classic role of a government, agency, or university board as setting policy, which then gets carried out by administrators. Many pages of detailed distinctions and limits can be written for a church wanting to use this approach for its own situation. Application is what makes the difference. Just putting words on sheets of paper will accomplish little. An inherent expectation is that the institution has a chief executive officer to oversee implementation. A question for any church is whether the senior pastor has such administrative capabilities. If the current one does, will the next one also? The alternative is to provide a staff position for someone with the competence and authority to work out the applications consistently.

SOME THEOLOGY

Of all the writers on Church Growth topics over the last thirty years, Christian Schwarz is by far the most theologically grounded—a German Lutheran, to boot. He shows evidence of insights from theologian Emil Brunner, who rearranged my thinking on truth as encounter, as discussed in chapter 2. Corollary to truth as personal encounter is church as event, not just structure. Schwarz's most theological discussion is in *Paradigm Shift in the Church: How Natural Church Development Can Transform Theological Thinking.*[9]

Two concepts stand out for me. 1. The "all-by-itself" principle is basic to change or growth in a congregation. The principle is rooted in the parable of the Growing Seed in the Gospel of Mark (Mark 4:26–29). Jesus says, "This is what the kingdom of God is like. A man scatters seed on the ground. Night and day, whether he sleeps or not, the seed sprouts and grows, though he does not know how. *All by itself* the soil produces grain." Like the seed in that little parable, the dynamics of self-growth are inherent in the seed of God's Word, through which the Holy Spirit works changes. This scriptural truth fits very well with the analogy of cultivating soil for the Holy Spirit, that is, breaking up the ground of customary ways of doing things, so that people gain new perspectives and so that it is easier for the Spirit to work new understandings and commitment in head and heart.

The "all-by-itself" principle is part of the "biotic potential," which refers basically to the capacity of living organisms to reproduce themselves. The apostle Paul thought in those terms when he made reference to the Corinthian congregation as a garden. He planted the seed, Apollos watered it, but God made it grow. The biological nature of a congregation is also well illustrated in Paul's description of how all the parts of a human body have to work together as the body of Christ (1 Corinthians 12:12–17).

2. Schwarz invites attention to "bipolar ecclesiology." He calls one the dynamic pole and the other the static pole. The dynamic pole is the world of encounters, events, happenings where the Spirit is moving in a live organism. The static pole is the world of organizational structure, institutions, formal doctrine in precise terms, unchanging tradition. The two need to be working together in constant tension. There is danger in either direction when the tension, with its change and uncertainties, is broken. Go too far to the dynamic side, and necessary forms, programs, and structures are considered irrelevant; often human sin spins spiritual encounters off into unwholesome and destructive relationships. Go too far to the static pole, and the proper doctrinal formulations and refined organizational rules are expected themselves to bring the right result; often the structure becomes impotent for lack of spiritual energy. The two kinds of effort need to be in interaction, often resulting in messiness and a level of uncertainty many leaders cannot accept. But some confusion has always has been a symptom of fruit-bearing churches, as the living body of Christ at a particular place expresses its fellowship, interests and energy at that time.

Such an understanding, drawn from Emil Brunner, lies behind the distinction I made in chapter 1 between going too far in the direction of objective truth or too far in the direction of subjective truth. Churches that value their doctrine and traditions usually don't have to worry about going too subjective. Those that should worry are congregations that lose their roots in the Word, overlook the depth of sin, and teach simplistic New Age fads. In turn, those that express the *objective* truth should worry about dwelling too much on the static pole, lest they become frozen in time. Brunner offers the image of orthodoxy as a frozen waterfall—mighty shapes of movement, yet no movement at all.[10]

There is no avoiding the fact that faithfulness to both Word and Spirit in paradoxical tension together is necessary for fruitfulness in the ministry of a congregation.

APPLICATION

Recognizing the concepts of seed and garden and of Word and Spirit has a very direct payoff in practical church leadership. Humans can plant the seed. But we can't force it to grow. Growth comes from the Spirit. What humans can do is limit that growth by presenting or failing to remove barriers. In simplest terms, a congregation can grow until there is no more seating capacity or not enough parking. Until services are added or buildings expanded or parking increased, the congregation will stop growing. On the other hand, adding parking does not automatically mean continued growth. It is a necessary condition, but sufficiency comes only from the Spirit.

A natural human tendency in all endeavors is for leaders to take credit for growth because of something they did or championed. This is understandable in business, but questionable in churches. From the social science perspective of organizational behavior, whether a certain cause is related to certain effect can only be ascertained by studying a number of organizations who try the same principle or method; then compare the outcomes.

This sort of rigorous research is almost totally absent from studies of church growth or decline, except for Schwarz's work behind Natural Church Growth. Otherwise, most of what we know comes from journalistic reports of "successful" congregations. Many are the stories of capable ministers and willing congregations who have tried to replicate the ministries offered by one or another featured congregation, but most often they do not have anything near the same results. The "real" story behind featured congregations is usually more complicated and has a few key turning points perhaps long forgotten.

My own take is that unusual church growth is a special blessing from the Holy Spirit working in special ways here or there. Pray for it. Recognize when the wind of growth has started to blow, and then work hard and take risks to remove barriers.

Royal Redeemer Lutheran Church in North Royalton, Ohio, where I serve, grew from 550 in attendance in 1994 to 1,000 in 2000, and leaders took many risks to remove barriers. We added staff, usually part-time, and expanded facilities in anticipation that sufficient funds would emerge. And they did. Some years we grew by 15% in offerings. But not well-known or appreciated is that in 1997 the Cleveland *Plain Dealer* ran a major front-page article on contemporary worship, featuring, with a large photograph, Royal Redeemer's services. Our attendance increased by about 150 within six months. The church also received an unsolicited, publicly anonymous gift of $1,150,000 for construction. No one could have planned or anticipated those two igniter events. About all you can do is give thanks, and then work really hard to be wise stewards of these special blessings. Recently we shifted staffing and took some financial risks to bring on board a worship pastor who could improve both contemporary and traditional worship experiences.

How will Royal Redeemer develop in coming years? Only God knows. Meanwhile we need to be faithful to our Lutheran teachings, to what we know about ministry in the builder model, and to better and more extensive ways of cultivating soil for the Holy Spirit.

QUESTIONS FOR DISCUSSION

1. What differences can you recognize between a church as a formal organization and a church as a fellowship?
2. What changes in formal organization of a congregation have you seen in your lifetime?

3. How comfortable are you with describing members involved in church ministries as "volunteers"?

4. In your thinking, what makes a Christian congregation a spiritual community different from any other social agency?

5. What has been your experience with the Natural Church Development model and assessment of Christian Schwarz?

6. Of the eight quality characteristics, what is your guess about which are the highest for your congregation and which are the lowest?

7. What is your reaction to the survey result that congregations of the LCMS score the lowest on the quality of loving relationships?

8. What has been your experience with the formal planning process in congregations you have been involved with?

9. What is your reaction to the theological principle of growth happening in a congregation "all by itself," as developed by Christian Schwarz?

10. Reflect on the "bipolar ecclesiology" of congregational life as a necessary tension between the dynamic pole of events and the static pole of structure and doctrine.

10

Overseeing
Fellowship Building

From the very beginning, Christian churches had overseers. In English they are called bishops. The Greek for bishop is *epi-scope,* or over-seer, equivalent to the Latin *super-visor.* In the Greek and Roman world of the earliest churches, these terms were used as much as the English *supervisor* is now in the everyday world of business and work organizations.

What did supervisors do in the work world then, including in the churches of builder Paul's time? They did about the same as supervisors do now on the factory floor or in offices. They looked after or watched over others; they carried responsibility for the work and actions of others; they tried to motivate and coordinate what others do.

The people who were overseen were called deacons in Greek and ministers in Latin. Those terms, too, were everyday words of the work and social world. *Minister* in Latin meant lesser one, as in *minor. Deacon* is the Greek word to describe waiting on tables. These servants helped overseers accomplish tasks.

Where would the minister of a congregation today fit into the organization of the congregations at Paul's time? The formal organization that shaped and protected each fellowship in those days was, understandably, simple and still developing. The fact is that in the writings of the New Testament there is no consistent structure and vocabulary. Three leader-type words were frequently used: First, the supervisors (*bishops*); second, helpers (*deacons*). The third in Greek was *presbyteros,* translated as "elder." Paul gave us qualifications for the first two roles, suggesting they were titles, which were specifically used in his greetings to the Philippians (1 Timothy 3:1–13; Philippians 1:1). His use of the third, *elder,* seems interchangeable with *overseer,* as was Peter's one use (Acts 20:17, 28; 1 Timothy 5:1, 2; Titus 1:5–7; 1 Peter 5:1). While the term could be used in its original sense for an older versus a younger man (1 Timothy 5:5; Hebrews 11:2), the extensive use by Luke in Acts as well as one occurrence in James (James 5:14) seem to be closer to our generic English term of "leader."

Add to these references the listing of spiritual giftedness of leadership and administration (1 Corinthians 12:28; Romans 12:8), and the observation is in order that there were plenty of leaders in Paul's congregations. But clearly there was also an overseer. Traditionally the bishop role was understood to include oversight of the teaching and doctrine of the church. Given Paul's emphasis on building up a fellowship, the role undoubtedly included supervision of the deacon/helpers and other leaders.

The bishop/overseer/supervisor role in the New Testament comes closest to the role of a builder minister in congregations today. The shepherd can be mostly the doer, with basic theological oversight. This helps explain why the "bishop" role in historic church bodies is confined to the overseer of many congregations. But the builder intends to get much of his work done through others. The supervisory role is unavoidable.

As the cohesiveness of community in a congregation decreases, the importance of purposeful efforts to build up fellowship increases. This chapter addresses how to be a good supervisor of many ministries. Insights from business administration can help.

PROVIDING STRUCTURE AND SUPPORT

The two basic behaviors for a supervisor are to provide Structure and offer Support.

Decades of research on leadership add up to the recognition of these two key variables as basic. They are also known as Task and Relationships. There is no one best combination. How much of which is needed depends mostly on the job maturity level of the worker. The circumstances are laid out best by Paul Hersey and Ken Blanchard.[1] Some readers may know them from their book *The One Minute Manager.*[2]

Providing Structure involves three behaviors: setting goals, guiding worker efforts, and providing technical assistance. Lack of sufficient structure is a major cause of worker dissatisfaction. As used here, worker can also mean a leader of somebody else's work. One implication of the church fellowship building model is that all program staff of a congregation should be considered leaders of the ministries of others.

Setting goals. Letting workers/leaders know the desired outcomes is the best way to start on structure. Then identify the significant steps and work flow. Beginning workers may need very explicit and detailed goals. Mature workers with sufficient training just need to be pointed in the right direction.

New staff and volunteers in a congregation are likely to need clear structure. If the supervisor (builder minister) does not know what that should be, then others with some experience need to be involved in setting the structure. This can often be done by finding workshops and conferences for the new worker/leader to attend. In this age of Google, there are usually plenty of options. One of the services a denomination can offer to congregations is to gather and make available information on all the learning opportunities reflective of that church body's ministries.

Of course, the starting assumption that the worker can figure out on her own what to do does make the supervisory job easier. But it is also a leading cause for dissatisfaction and turnover in staff and volunteer leader positions.

Guiding efforts. Checking regularly is part of supervision. At any given time, what should the priorities be? What feedback is there from earlier efforts?

In a congregation, this looks like regular meetings of the workers with whoever is guiding them. Close supervision—micromanaging with daily checking and very specific instructions—can be annoying. But talking about the job once or twice a year is too little. New workers need more check-in time than do experienced ones. A builder minister who is supervising others simply must make time available on a planned and regular basis. All should have a monthly time, and some may need more frequent interaction with the supervisor.

Providing technical assistance. The provision of necessary tools, supplies and work conditions is basic. Workers typically rank "receiving enough help and equipment to get the job done" at the top of the list of what is important to them.

In churches there should be provision for workspace and storage. If learning materials are involved, the minister should have suggestions. A frequent complaint of staff members is that they can't find enough people to participate in the ministries they want to do. Clarifying up front that finding them is part of the staff member's job helps. But getting members engaged in a ministry may be part of a larger problem with spiritual gifts administration, and this issue needs attention at the highest levels.

Offering Support involves three basic behaviors: creating a feeling of approval, recognizing individuality, and providing fair treatment. While workers anywhere need to have structure, they also need supportive relationships. Such relationships help prevent frustration and feelings of dissatisfaction. They also keep a worker or leader committed to the ministry.

Creating a sense of approval. Supervisors can communicate approval to those they work with in many ways—taking an active interest in them as individuals, listening to their problems, giving praise when justified, showing tolerance when mistakes are made. What is most important is the person's psychological perception of approval. Approval can be transmitted with courtesy and trust. But what one worker perceives as trust may be taken by someone else as a discouraging disinterest in what they are doing. As ever, it is the supervisor's role to adjust.

Churches typically have loose structures that make it hard to know just what the worker/leader is doing. Being aware enough to recognize where the person has made extra effort provides opportunity to give the best approval of "well done." That means a lot more than routine clichés of niceness. When poorly led, congregations can often fail to show meaningful appreciation for those working on their behalf.

Recognizing individuality. Showing personal interest in subordinates individually helps form supportive relationships. Often the more that supervisors learn about their co-workers, the more they can understand difficulties on the job. Interest can be shown by knowing about hobbies, or favorite activities of their family, or future ambitions. It also extends to the willingness to listen. This involves also being visibly available and open to talk.

Supportive relationships should be easier to provide in a church than in many work places. But sometimes there are spiritual difficulties that cannot be openly talked about. Nevertheless, conscious efforts need to be made to identify something personal workers are comfortable sharing in front of others. Gentle teasing about something safe can accomplish a lot.

Providing fair treatment. Workers have a strong need to feel that the organization is treating them fairly, especially in the way they are assigned work, compensated, given attention, and provided with workspace or office. This does not mean that everyone has to receive exactly the same treatment. Most important is that decisions are made on grounds recognized as legitimate according to the needs of the organization.

Ministers, like all supervisors, have their personal likes and dislikes about those they work with. The tendency is to spend time mostly with those we like, and this can be seen as unfair. Beyond the office, congregations are also political networks. Everyone needs to feel his or her needs are getting a fair hearing. This takes time and initiative spent especially with those who are less visible. Again, most important is that all perceive that minister/supervisor's decisions about time and attention are based on legitimate grounds for the good of the congregation.

COMMUNICATING LIKE AN ADMINISTRATOR

Let's take the supervisor role a step further. Consider the overall role of the administrator of a formal organization. It is hard to build church fellowship among members who also are part of corporate culture of modern America without working through the formal structure of a congregation. For most, that is their expectation. Thus it is hard to be a builder minister today without thinking like an administrator. The alternatives are: a) settle for small building projects, or b) find someone else who can help with administrative perspective and oversight.

The Old Testament gives us the model of a great administrator, Nehemiah. In every possible sense he was a builder, both in rebuilding the physical wall around Jerusalem and thereby also in rebuilding the Jewish community in Jerusalem. After the Jews were taken in captivity to Babylon, Jerusalem with its temple was left in ruins. Jewish Nehemiah, a high official with King Artaxerxes in Susa, accepted an invitation from the remnant to remove their disgrace by rebuilding the walls of Jerusalem. With the blessing of the king—including building materials—Nehemiah showed up at the wall in 445 BC. After inspecting the situation for three days he came up with a plan. He communicated with four kinds of messages.[3]

First, he simply reviewed the problem with the Jerusalem leaders and *stated the clear mission and vision* for them: Let's rebuild the wall.

Second, he let *action messages* speak the loudest. Within two days, all those living in Jerusalem found themselves hauling stones and beams and witnessing progress. Nehemiah confidently and visually showed them what to do. They learned by doing, not by talking.

Action messages in a congregation today perhaps speak the loudest of all. What messages are being sent by current actions, especially if those consist of only one hour a week of passive involvement in worship? Scolding will not accomplish much.

Highlighting and endorsing ministries beyond Sunday would help. When worship leaders do not give prime time to announcements about what members are actually doing in ministries, a church is missing a fundamental way to model fellowship and therefore to build it up. A great way to start a new mission is for the pastor or other senior leader to announce, for instance, "I am going Thursday evening to help teach English to Muslims along Lorain Ave. Who will come with me?"

Third, Nehemiah buttressed these actions messages with *informal group messages*. He organized the residents to work within their natural family groupings, as described in the third chapter of the Old Testament book Nehemiah. He worked through the natural group leaders and let them fill in the specifics in their own way.

Today the grapevine is usually at work in any active organization. Get to know the informal subsets of participants. When they have the facts wrong, move to clarify the situation. Good administration would get controversial actions publicly explained as soon as possible. Go out of your way to spend time with key people in the informal networks. I once had a pastor in a course who complained that a group of his elders met for breakfast on certain mornings at a specific restaurant; he was worried they were undercutting him. My response was to point out that the restaurant is a public building. Go join their breakfast on occasion. It would be hard for them to say that the pastor is not welcome. What an opportunity for this pastor to sell his agenda. To do so had not occurred to him.

Fourth, Nehemiah called for *formal agreements* to head off conflict. When issues of injustice emerged (the workers became aggrieved against the nobles and officials) he confronted nobles and officials for their injustice (charging interest on loans) and insisted they give back what they had taken. He formalized their promise as a pledge and made a ceremony of it. Fully aired and settled with a formal agreement, the work continued with united effort. Later, after the wall was finished, Ezra and Nehemiah called on each major family grouping to publicly make and sign a written pledge to honor the Sabbath and their Jewish heritage as well as to make specific offerings. This was all part of a huge formal ceremony.

The formal agreement of a pledge can be powerful today, too. Many congregations are used to asking their members for a financial pledge for the new year. At the end of the year, they then report to each donor the amount received. Granted, this is primarily for tax purposes of reporting charitable contributions. But think of the message sent when only dollars are important enough to track and report. What would be the impact of asking for a written pledge about frequency of worship attendance and hours of Bible study or service projects in the new year? At a minimum, it says these are important values. Certainly such reporting would take a lot of work. But maybe God has gifted the congregation with several people who would regard such computer work as their special contribution to the good of the congregation.

There was yet another kind of message involved in rebuilding Jerusalem. The messenger was the prophet Ezra, whose words are told in the Old Testament book of Ezra that comes just before the book of Nehemiah. Ezra was the senior preacher and spiritual leader. He concentrated on the spiritual preparation for the Jerusalem residents—prayer, fasting, repentance. He laid the spiritual foundation, a prerequisite for Nehemiah's successful building project.

The called minister of a congregation today certainly has the Ezra role of spiritual leader. Should that expand to include the Nehemiah role of administrator? It almost has to if the minister intends to move from being a shepherd to a builder of a church's fellowship. If the minister is not the architect leading the formulation of clear and specific mission and vision, who will be? If the minister does not plan and communicate many kinds of consistent messages (preaching, modeling, using small groups, shaping formal agreements), who will be? The alternative is to hire or raise up a leader with high-level leader capabilities. But then be willing to take guidance from him or her, as Ezra clearly did under the leadership of Nehemiah.

In whatever form, communication is basic to supervising. Think of the changes in communication technology since the apostle Paul's times. Then it would have been almost all face-to-face conversation with fellow workers. Paul had no office to retreat to; nor did he have a favorite chair to read in. He was either making tents or interacting with others in the church. Writing memos was difficult because of the expense of papyrus or parchment. So he just talked to people and explained his thinking.

Since then we have had the "progress" of desks, telephones, typewriters, copy machines, word processing, answering machines, faxes, and now widespread e-mail and Web sites. Except for the last two, I am not sure how all this technology has really improved communication with fellow workers beyond what Paul was doing. There are just too many words floating around; it is hard for anyone to sort out what is important.

I like Web sites because they are always handy as a reference for an individual to get answers to his or her questions. The most teachable moment is when someone has a question. Helping them find an answer right away on their own is certainly better than expecting them to find the right person and the right time to ask, which might be weeks later. E-mail is also good because it is so easy for fellow workers to keep updating each other. Think of how it increases a supervisor's opportunities to give a fifteen-second response of acknowledgement or thanks. It can help close the communication loop almost as well as being face to face. Ministers who think about the supervisory role discussed in this chapter may well hesitate because it can all seem so bureaucratic. Thanks to the very latest technology, we can regain much of the simplicity of Paul's fellowship-building communication.

RAISING UP LEADERS BY THE 2-2-2 PRINCIPLE

2 Timothy, chapter 2, verse 2: "The things you have heard me say in the presence of many witnesses entrust to reliable people, who will also be qualified to teach others."

The apostle Paul gave this encouragement to his protégé Timothy. What do you think Paul had in mind with "the things you heard me say" which are to be taught to others?

When this passage is interpreted by teachers and scholars, the tendency is to think of theological content mostly in the form of doctrine. Indeed, Paul did this in Romans 1–11 and in other foundation-laying passages in his letters. But he taught a lot more than that. Did he think of himself primarily as a theologian or as a church builder? I vote for the latter. His letters are mostly occasional—written on the occasion of responding to a problem or a need in a specific congregation. His aim was usually to reduce conflict or to challenge them to higher unified action. Theory was important to the extent it helped build up a congregation.

It is instructive to observe the development of Paul's thinking about congregational leaders. For that we need a timeline of his ministry and writings, something that in Biblical scholarship is complicated and controversial. I accept and will follow the one set forth in the *Concordia Study Bible*.[4]

DEVELOPMENT OF PAUL'S APPROACH TO LEADER DEVELOPMENT

The passage at hand from 2 Timothy is Paul's last writing, done during his final imprisonment in Rome about 67/68 AD. He is passing on his accumulated wisdom and encouragement from twenty years of founding, leading and supervising congregations. He has clearly recognized the importance of raising up and training leaders within a congregation. His was no equivalent of a TV ministry to the church at large. He led congregation by congregation. He says: Timothy, take what you heard from me in so many situations and commend (delegate) it to faithful people who will be competent to teach it to others. In other words, concentrate on raising up and equipping leaders for the expanding number of churches.

Four years earlier in his first letter to Timothy, chapter 3, Paul identified the kind of leaders he had in mind. He laid out basic qualifications for the overseers (bishops) and for the helpers (deacons) who are to be overseen. In chapter 5 of that letter, he commends double honor to "elders who direct the affairs of the church, especially those whose work is preaching and teaching." Elders appear to be the larger group, of which some are overseers and others preach and teach. My own take is that the Greek *presbyter* (elder) is equivalent to our general term *leader* today; *elder* did not primarily describe age. Among those leaders there are differing gifts and roles. This is the structure Paul had in mind as he looked back on his building up of congregations.

To see the development of his thinking we need to go back to the two places where Paul stayed long enough to have daily involvement in building up a church plant. First, he was in Corinth for a year and a half (51–52 AD) on his second missionary journey. Then on his third journey, he spent perhaps three years (53–55 AD) in Ephesus. From there he went back to Greece, including Corinth, where problems of those churches were very much on his mind. Ending this third journey, on his way back to Jerusalem in 56/57 AD, he stopped near Ephesus and met with those elders he had come to know so well. Arrested soon after arriving in Jerusalem, Paul then spent years in prison in Caesarea and in Rome. As far as we know, his church planting days were over. Thus out of circulation, he had to rely on others to build up the churches. How providential it was that those leaders he had raised up had no alternative but to become themselves strong church leaders, who in turn knew how to raise up others.

To understand Paul's experience and thinking during those crucial years of 51–57 AD, we have his two letters to the Corinthians plus his letter to the Romans, whom he had not yet visited. He wrote his letter to the Ephesians from his imprisonment in Rome just a few years after he left them. By that time he had worked out the broad features of his thinking about church leaders as stated in the Ephesians passage: Get fellow members aligned for ministry of building up the body of Christ, until that congregation becomes mature and reaches to the very heights of the fullness of Christ.

Paul was not always focused on new leaders. Luke tells us (Acts 18:11) that in Corinth he stayed a year and a half teaching people the "word of God"—basic teachings about God and the new covenant. Telling us about Paul a year later in Ephesus (Acts 19:9), Luke's vocabulary has changed as he describes how Paul took the "disciples" and had "dialogue" with them in the school of Tyrannus. He no longer was teaching people in general, but now had his own disciples with whom he carried on daily dialogue.

Presumably that dialogue branched out into practical affairs of leading the house churches that were basic to the spreading of the Christian church in big metropolitan areas. Many of the disciples were probably house church leaders. Many probably helped plant the other six of the seven churches described in Revelation 2–3; all are within about a hundred miles of Ephesus. At that same time in Ephesus, he was wrestling with and writing about all the problems showing up in the fellowships of Corinth. Undoubtedly these problems provided examples for the Ephesus dialogues. What an intense period those few years in Ephesus were for conceptualizing and working out structure for those very early churches. Just as the disciples of Jesus became the first generation of leaders, Paul's disciples went on to become key members of the Gentile second-generation leaders.

Luke (Acts 20:17, 28) tells us that by the time Paul left Ephesus in 57 AD, some of the Ephesus disciples had become elders and overseers. It is interesting to note that three years later when Paul wrote to the Philippians, he addressed specifically their overseers and deacons. The greetings of his earlier letters were to the "saints" or "the churches" in general.

Note that it is in the first letter to the Corinthians (from Ephesus) that Paul writes the great chapter 12 about using the gifts of the Spirit in the body of Christ, describing more eloquently what he must have been doing among them in practice. Then, soon after, he applied that same framework also in the letter from Corinth (Cenchreae) to the Romans in chapter 12. When several years later from Rome he wrote to the Ephesians the letter that has so many key statements about church leadership, he almost certainly was describing in general terms what he had already taught them in practice about being joined together by every ligament as a holy temple of the Lord, growing and building itself up in love.

RAISING UP CHURCH LEADERS IN SUDAN

It has been my privilege to observe firsthand an application of Paul's 2-2-2 principle to building up a church body today. This is the Evangelical Lutheran Church in Sudan. It was founded in 1994 by Andrew Elisa, a Sudanese who had been in a high position with the Anglican Church of Sudan but felt drawn toward Lutheran teachings. After some initial training at Concordia Theological Seminary in Fort Wayne, Indiana, he began his work in the capital city of Khartoum among refugees of the decades-long war in southern Sudan. I was part of a team teaching his lay leaders in 1999. At that time he had twelve congregations functioning in various parts of the country. That same summer, he was ordained by officials of the Board for Mission Services of The Lutheran Church—Missouri Synod, who also gave recognition to the Evangelical Lutheran Church of Sudan as a partner church body.

The son of an important tribal chief in southern Sudan, Rev. Elisa followed up his relationships with refugees scattered also beyond Khartoum. When peace came to southern Sudan in the early 2000s (the conflict in Darfur is in western Sudan), he moved his base to southern Sudan and started planting churches in dozens of villages newly made accessible with the removal of land mines from the roads. His usual approach was to enter a village, gather a group and then preach and teach for several weeks. He could have stayed longer to build up that congregation; like Paul so often did, he moved on to the next village. Of course a leader has to be left behind. Recognizing and raising up an elder is an important part of that initial work. By latest count, the Evangelical Lutheran Church in Sudan has 100 congregations with 15,000 members. The church I serve has provided support to build a sanctuary for two different villages at the bargain rate of $5,000 each.

It does not take much insight to realize the tension inherent in this approach to church planting. How good are the new leaders who will develop and guide these village congregations? Ideally they should be well trained first, before taking on responsibilities. But the mission opportunities are unique to the current time and place. So the challenge is to bring training to them while they function as leaders. For this purpose, Rev. Elisa has had to develop a structure for oversight. This involves evangelists who work directly with four or five congregations and deacons and deaconesses who function within the village. The longer-term need is to develop a seminary in Baguga in south Sudan with ongoing training that will prepare the most capable for ordination as ministers who will oversee regions of the church body. Quite rightfully, Rev. Andrew Elisa is called Bishop Elisa.

The apostle Paul would recognize the method immediately. It is application of the principle in 2 Timothy 2:2: "The things you have heard me say in the presence of many witnesses entrust to reliable people who will also be qualified to teach others."

An intriguing question is what content should be entrusted to these new leaders to teach to others. It is probably a lot less than is taught in the four years of college and four more years of seminary expected for Lutheran ministers in America. Another intriguing question is whether the training brought to functioning church leaders will produce better results than first providing years of academic preparation before taking on leadership responsibilities. In any event, the helper role of deacon and evangelist under supervision is crucial to building up the new Lutheran church body in Sudan.

SUPERVISORS AND HELPERS TODAY

What should we do with the historic deacon role in churches today?

For classic shepherd ministry in a shepherd congregation, a formalized helper/deacon role is not a compelling necessity. Only when the congregation gets big does the minister need help doing the basic pastoral functions of preaching, teaching, leading worship, and caring for the ill and aged. Then a second pastor might be added, or perhaps a student minister in an internship.

But for the builder minister, the helper/deacons are crucial. The difference is in the theory that relationships within the fellowship no longer need primarily to go through the minister. Other leaders are expected to take responsibility for a flow of some of the fellowship relationships that will happen primarily through them. Instead of the minister being the hub of the big wheel of the whole congregation, helpers are expected to become hubs of sub-wheels. This makes possible the development of more and stronger relationships that are basic to fellowship building. The smaller hubs themselves are then leaders for those in their groupings.

Consider, again, the builder image Paul used to describe himself to the Corinthians. His ministry was as an *architekton* in the original Greek. The customary translation is a master builder. But why not stay with the literal translation as the architect we know today? The Greek word has two parts: *archi-tekton*. The *archi* means originating or master. The *tekton* we have in the English technician, who does the hands-on work. Think carpenter. But of course today there are also plumbers, electricians, heating specialists, dry-wall tapers, and other specialists in the construction trades. It is with the increase of specialists and of the great variety of building materials that an intermediate-level builder has emerged in the last century—the contractor, who finds and schedules the hands-on workers as well as delivery of the materials. So we have three kinds of builders: the hands-on workers (carpenters), the contractor, and the architect.

Builder ministry today needs to function on all three levels. In *shepherd* ministry the pastor does all the hands-on work of ministry, in which case the ordained pastor's role is carpenter ministry. Carpenter ministers and passive shepherd congregations usually get along quite well. The minister does the important work and the laypeople support that.

Much of the work of builder ministers is contracting—finding others to take on important roles and then supervising them with structure and support. Those who have taken on a basic ministry would be the helpers in the deacon role. Of necessity, builder ministers spend a major part of their time as supervisors. This duty belongs to the overseer or bishop role described by Paul.

In congregations where traditions are still functioning well, the congregation does not need an architect. They can work from the same set of drawings or expectations that have been in place for decades. From experience they know what the outcome should look like. It is when the old drawings no longer produce the same results that there is need to consider a new approach. This is when maintenance turns into building ministry. This is when new mission and vision need to be worked out. This is architect's work.

What might some helper or deacon roles look like today? The deaconess role has long been recognized for mercy ministries. But in many traditions, there is no comparable role for men. Meanwhile, many other helping roles have emerged: teachers in Christian Day Schools, lay ministers, directors of Christian education, or of outreach, or of family life, or of small groups, or of assimilation. Often leaders with these various roles are described as being "on staff." Large churches today may have ten to fifteen people "on staff," besides the office support staff. They are basically all deacon helpers, and churches could use that title with its special dignity more frequently. Some even get licensed for Word and Sacrament ministry in special situations.

One of the limitations that can too easily happen is for staff members to think they themselves are supposed to do the important ministry in their area. For expanding churches, the challenge is to help these staffers see themselves as motivating and coordinating the ministries of yet others.

A constant question is where the boundary is between ordained ministry and the other helper or support ministries. From a builder perspective of expanding ministries, what can be done only by the ordained should be kept as minimal as possible. From the shepherd perspective the opposite is more likely; what the ordained can do is broadened as much as possible.

The builder model of ministry would recognize a three-part distinction of members in a congregation: the overseer, the deacons, and everybody else. Church bodies with state church backgrounds from Europe generally have a two-part distinction: clergy and laity or ordinary people.

After this overview of Paul's approach to building up congregations, the three-part approach seems more Biblical. A challenge for church bodies that want to support growing congregations is to provide more explicitly for the role and status of deacon for those ministering in between the ordained and everyone else. Qualifications for recognition could be determined and educational course requirements set

MINISTRY	MINISTRY
Done by All, with many leaders	**Done by** ordained and commissioned
Pastor As Overseer	**Pastor** As doer
Power: Holy Spirit	**Power:** Knowledge and order

up at district level without the need for college accreditation and degrees. This could be more easily done now through Internet-based distance education.

QUESTIONS FOR DISCUSSION

1. What have you envisioned to be the work of the early church supervisors (bishops)?
2. Share examples of how you have provided structure for someone working in a congregation and how you usually provide support.
3. Do you have any thoughts to share on how fairness is perceived to be so important in a congregation?
4. How have you used Nehemiah in your own thinking and teaching on church leadership?
5. Can you identify several informal power centers in your congregation?
6. What do you think is the best improvement in communication technology in the last half century?
7. How have you thought about and taught Paul's 2–2–2 principle in 2 Timothy 2:2: "The things you have heard me say in the presence of many witnesses entrust to reliable people, who will also be qualified to teach others"?
8. How have you envisioned the early church relationships between bishop, elder and deacon?
9. What is your reaction to Bishop Andrew Elisa's church planting strategy in Sudan?
10. How important is it to you to raise up and encourage more deacons in your congregation?

11

The Transition Process

"It isn't the changes that do you in, it's the transitions."[1]

Change makes church leadership so much harder now. It happens today whether you want it or not. The definition of change here refers to what happens around a person, or an organization, or a congregation; call it the context or the environment. Transition refers to how internal adjustments are made to external changes.

Every congregation faces changes of many sorts. The issue is how to cope with them.

The easiest changes to spot are in communication technology and in the generation that has grown up with new technology. High-quality audio and visual systems for churches are now available at close to home-owner prices. An overview of those options began in chapter 4 on the Builder's Toolbox. If members of a congregation were willing to contribute just a tenth of what they spend on their home systems (stereo receiver, speakers, CD storage, DVD player, big-screen TV, computer), most congregations could easily purchase entry-level equipment, including a video projector, to do multimedia presentations in the sanctuary.

In view of new communication realities, congregations have several options. The easiest transition is toward better wireless microphones, mixer board, and speakers. Few object to having the sound experience be more comfortable, just like few resist air-conditioning. Leave the question of cost aside for the moment. More difficult is a transition to adding a screen and projector with video and PowerPoint content to worship in the sanctuary. This is a very noticeable change to the context of the individual worshiper's experience.

The easiest of all responses to changes in affordable technology is to do nothing. What was good enough for decades in the past should be good enough for the future. A church that ignores such opportunities is making a transition whether or not it realizes it. That congregation is moving further out of the mainstream of attractiveness to potential new members. Remember, higher expectations and increased competition are basic to what makes the environment for churches so much harder today.

For the generation of young adults that have grown up on computers and the Internet, the absence of basic new technology sends a strong signal that this congregation is really not forward looking. Having even a simple Web site may not mean much to seniors, but it does communicate that the congregation is at least trying.

The transition to using some of the latest financially feasible communication capabilities is much more difficult than just finding the money and being willing to hear and see the results. Getting communication done well on both the sending and receiving sides takes time and experience. Early attempts are usually not very excit-

118

ing. I shudder to think of our use of PowerPoint in sermons twelve years ago. It was primitive and often confusing. But you have to start somewhere. Like most things, it takes practice to get good.

When considering the cost in terms of equipment, time, and confusion, think of the alternate cost of not beginning this transition. Every year that goes by without upgrading communication means a congregation is falling further behind in ability to attract and hold young people and families. Ministry, indeed, is just plain harder now.

But remember a basic point from the chapter on the role of the Holy Spirit in church growth. Insufficient parking, for instance, is a barrier to growth. But just because you add more parking does not guarantee growth. It is necessary, but the sufficiency comes through action of the Spirit. So also with communication technology. Absence of new ways becomes a barrier for young people. But more proficiency does not automatically bring growth. It does, however, increase the chances for the Holy Spirit to bless communication that attracts and builds up relationships with a newer generation.

This illustration of changing technology is an apparent and relatively simple example of change beyond the congregation that calls for some sort of transition within to adapt to it. Other simple illustrations are a leaky roof or worn-out boiler— changes calling for a transition to a higher amount of member financial support to the congregation. Failure to make such a shift means the building will deteriorate rapidly, and probably with it, the congregation.

A more basic and compelling change is a relative absence of children and young adults in a congregation. Does such a fact call for a shift in how ministries are done? One shift might be toward ministries oriented to young families. Another might be toward more offerings for seniors. Changing nothing is a transition toward a weaker congregation with a limited future. One does hear of rapidly declining churches where the main motivation of key members is to keep the church going long enough to be available for their own funerals. What vestige is left of commendable faithfulness, let alone fruitfulness?

Sometimes a congregation's response may be to increase advertising in hopes of "filling the pews" so that the budget can be maintained. Better advertising and printed outreach might well be helpful. But if the motivation is to just to keep the numbers up, little will probably come of it. A big part of the overall challenge today is to actually deliver spiritual benefits a visitor can readily recognize. Working on a transition to "deliver the goods" better is probably a more productive place to start. Can members learn new ways to better show love and care for each other and especially for visitors (see chapter 8)? Can they make better transitions toward ways of worshipping that, as the apostle Paul says, would lead a visitor to "fall down and worship God, exclaiming 'God is really among you!' " (1 Corinthians 14:25)?

Stay a bit more with the issue of worship forms. Maybe one congregation is quite happy with its traditional liturgy. But neighboring congregations are shifting to "contemporary" worship. A small-town pastor once told me that all congregations of the denomination should be forced to do the same liturgical forms so that neighboring congregations would not draw off his members. Staying with tradition, he was at a competitive disadvantage. But that is just the point of the new hard environment for churches, even in the Upper Midwest. Expectations are higher and competition is increasing.

AVOIDING TRANSITION PITFALLS

The biggest pitfall to adapting new ways of responding to change is conflict. Some want to do new or different forms of ministry. Others like the old ways as they are. A second pitfall is failure to look beyond the personal interests of the present membership.

Conflict brings stress. As a profession, ministers have an especially high proportion of practitioners who are conflict adverse; they don't want to deal with conflict and try to reduce it as quickly as possible. The easiest path forward is to leave things as they are. A better path forward is for church leaders to learn and then teach the change process so potential conflict can be less painful.

Conflict begins when sides are drawn between "us" and "them." "Us" would be the ones for change; "them" are all those who resist. Conflict worsens when rational discussion is displaced by strong emotions. This is also when conflict becomes painful and starts doing damage in the fellowship.

Resistance can turn emotional when the transition under discussion carries a lot of emotional attachment, especially as a symbol for an understanding of "their" church that would be discarded. Resistance becomes more entrenched when those who oppose the idea begin to sense that they personally are being ignored or devalued.

On the issue of worship, a lady wrote to me about how she remembered as a kid feeling sorry for the few old Germans dressed in dark clothes who attended the German service early Sunday mornings. I have the same picture in mind from my home church through the 1950s. Life had passed them by. Much to her disappointment, she, with her commitment to liturgical worship, was beginning to feel like them—cast off and left behind. It would take an unusually strong personality to avoid resistance, whatever the specifics are, and even if traditional worship remains in the early service.

The natural reaction of advocates of change is to avoid dealing with the "them" who resist. There are often many differences in addition to the issue at hand. Avoidance is exactly the wrong thing to do. The challenge is to demonstrate that those on the other side of the issue are still valued personally. This can be done, at a minimum, by giving them time and attention, preferably individually. A visit or a telephone call to explain the proposal and seek their reaction goes a long way, as does simple courtesy. When they feel they have been heard and appreciated, their resistance may still remain, but the emotional entrenchment and opposition will be lessened.

Maintaining integrity in the relationships of a congregation is part of Paul's call to love one another. In addition to respecting the value of those who resist, remaining trustworthy is basic. Potential painful conflict is considerably reduced when members trust the minister who is leading them. Such trust has to be earned and can easily be squandered by arbitrary self-serving actions. Pastoral wisdom lies in discerning which kinds of changes can be made with little opposition and which need to be carefully processed. When we at Royal Redeemer changed the Sunday second sanctuary service from 11:15 am to 10:00 a.m., the senior pastor called all the regular attendees of that service and solicited their reaction to the proposal. The change was made with no disruption.

Another pitfall is failure to look beyond the personal interests of the present membership. Then the struggle is like that of an ordinary social club considering only the preferences of the members. Transitions are much easier when there is a goal beyond the fellowship. Social psychologists call this having a "superordinate goal."

In churches we call that the mission beyond self-maintenance. Existing for the benefit of others is not something that comes easily to those who gather together with normal human motivations. Ultimately, strong mission motivation comes through the work of the Holy Spirit. Hosting the Spirit is basic to spiritual leadership.

Being in mission really does work to improve congregational life. A district mission development counselor, Gary Thies, tells story after story of working with small, rural Midwest congregations that were struggling and in conflict before they adopted a specific foreign missionary to support financially and to offer their encouragement and prayers. Looking beyond themselves really did help them renew and revitalize themselves.[2]

UNDERSTANDING THE CHANGE PROCESS

Organizational development consultants Cynthia Scott and Dennis Jaffe present a helpful framework for understanding the transitions through change.[3] They differentiate what happens externally in the environment from what happens internally in the self. The second dimension differentiates a focus on the past from a focus on the future. Put these two dimensions together and you have a four-cell outline of movement through four stages. Scott and Jaffe label them as denial, resistance, exploration, and commitment.[4]

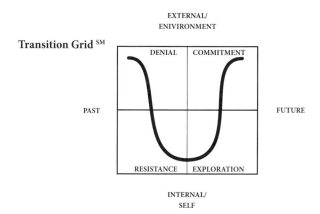

Transition Grid SM

EXTERNAL/ENIVIRONMENT

DENIAL | COMMITMENT

PAST | FUTURE

RESISTANCE | EXPLORATION

INTERNAL/SELF

During change, people focus on the past and *deny* the change. Next, they go through a period of preoccupation, wondering where they stand and how they will be affected. This is normally where *resistance* occurs. As they enter the *exploration* and *commitment* phases, they start to look toward the future and the opportunities it can bring.

Denial is the first stage, which is really the first stage of any grief brought about by a loss. Transition involves loss. The anxiety may be about loss of security, competence, relationships or sense of direction. If these feelings are ignored or suppressed, they will intensify the resistance. Appropriate action is to sell the problem, perhaps by pointing out how the cost of not changing may be greater than the cost of making the change. Be sure to allow time for ideas and changes to sink in.

Resistance occurs when people have moved through denial and begin to experience self-doubt, anger, depression, anxiety, and frustration. In churches this may show up as low morale, expression of negative feelings or even the departure of some people. Researchers tell us people resist change for four basic reasons:

- A desire not to lose something of value.
- A misunderstanding of the change and its implications.
- A belief that the change does not make sense.
- A low tolerance for change in their psychological makeup.[5]

Reggie McNeal observes that too many pastors think phases 1 and 2 (denial and resistance) are not normal, and they take the negative feelings personally.[6]

Wise leadership addresses resistance by letting it vent, by communicating extensively, by including potential resistors in the planning process, and by providing emotional support to help them say good-bye to the old.

Exploration takes place in the third phase, when opportunities start emerging. Energy is released, and the focus is again on the future. Often this phase looks like chaos as people try to figure out new responsibilities, search for new ways to relate to each other and wonder how the "new" will work. It is important to give verbal and organizational permission for people to quit doing things that do not yield the desired results. This phase can be exciting and exhilarating, yielding powerful new bonds of relationships.

In the **commitment** phase, the congregation is ready to focus on a plan, to buy into the vision, to build action plans that will achieve the mission. Church members are willing to learn new ways of behaving with each other; they have renegotiated their roles and expectations. This is the time to develop a mission statement with long-term goals.[7]

Social psychologist Kurt Lewin reduces these four phases to three: Unfreezing, Changing and Refreezing. Changes cannot happen if the old ways are still frozen. The participants need to know that there are problems with these ways. One cannot continue to reinforce the old and then turn around one day and say, "Now we have to switch to these new ways." Naturally there will be resistance. Once made, the new ways then need to be refrozen in the sense that they are done consistently.

OBSERVATIONS ON INTRODUCING CHANGE IN CHURCHES

Based on work done by Lyle Schaller, church consultant and author Reggie Mc-Neal offers some observations on how to introduce change, especially in churches:

1. Seek to change by addition whenever possible.

2. Avoid a vote to change. Only rarely do changes succeed that pass by narrow margins on the floor of the church business meeting. People will tend to vote against change when you ask them to replace what they know with something they have little experience with.

3. Present proposed changes as an experiment rather than a permanent change, if that is truly the case. This allows the change to be introduced with less resistance.

4. Count only positive votes. Try not to give people who do not have a stake in an issue veto power over the decision.

5. Implement the initial components of an overall strategy that will: (a) most likely be seen as a success, and (b) will require relatively few changes. The idea is to create momentum and a sense of being in a winning enterprise.

6. Whenever possible, make only one change at a time. As the number of changes goes up, so does the anxiety.

7. Changes are most likely to be initiated and implemented if they originate in an ad hoc committee. Standing committees are not designed to be incubators of innovation. It is better to appoint a task force or special group to creatively deal with a challenge or opportunity.

8. Four types of support are needed to insure the acceptability of change:

   a. the senior pastor, who must be in favor of major changes or they will lack legitimization.

   b. those who will turn the plan into reality, including workers.

   c. those who allocate resources, including calendar, money, and space.

   d. the passive neutrality of those holding veto power.[8]

AN INNOVATIVE CONGREGATION

A congregation going through transitions is becoming an innovative congregation—doing things new to them. They are changing their church culture and developing a new "ethos."

Reggie McNeal reports also on characteristics of innovative congregations.[9] While the basic energy and growth outcomes of a congregation are determined by movement of the Holy Spirit, these characteristics themselves are outcomes that human leaders can work toward. Or put differently, the absence of these characteristics shows where to focus human energy on moving toward the positive. In the process the congregation needs to become better at cultivating their soil for their Holy Spirit.

Innovative congregations reflect:
- A leader who genuinely loves God and loves the people, and this love is obvious.
- Positive up-building language.
- Members are aware of the congregation's contribution to their personal growth.
- An inspiring worship experience.
- A care-centered infrastructure.
- A building that exudes warmth and welcome.
- A belief that the best days of the congregation are now and to come.
- An expectancy that God will show up.
- A passion for excellence.
- A staff that loves each other and their work.
- A vital prayer ministry.
- Positive ministry experiences.
- An orientation to process.
- Noncompetitive diversity.

LET REASON PREVAIL

When tradition no longer adequately serves to determine how a ministry will be done in the future, church leaders do well to lean heavily on rational planning as the approach toward figuring out transitions that are appropriate. Otherwise they are left to negotiate personal preferences that are likely to be emotionally charged. In twenty-first century America, most church members would accept the starting general value that reason should prevail in the congregation's approach to the future.

There are at least two characteristics of rational decision-making. One is that you don't know you have the best until it is compared to at least two alternatives. Otherwise you only know you have a good solution, not the better or best. The second characteristic is using cause-and-effect reasoning. If you want outcome A, then you should try steps 1 and 2. The limits of such reasoning in churches I will comment more on later.

STRATEGIC PLANNING GUIDE

In ten years of teaching a doctor of ministry course, I had about two hundred pastors do their course report on their plan to lead their congregation after returning home. Most used one or the other of the following two models. The first is a strategic planning guide, which was mentioned in the planning portion of chapter 10 on organizing. The second is a force field analysis.

A full-page version of this Strategic Planning Guide is found on p. 131.

For strategic planning, picture a large writing surface with five columns that need to be filled in with SWOT-S. In column 1 are the **S**trengths (e.g., good building,

Strategic Planning Guide
for _____ Church

I. IDENTIFYING SWOTS

CURRENT CHURCH RESOURCES		POSSIBLE NEEDS TO ADDRESS		POSSIBLE MAJOR GOALS
Strengths	Weaknesses	Opportunities	Threats	Satisfactions to Offer

II. EVALUATING ALTERNATIVES
Importance of Outcomes

Feasibility with resources

Fit with the congregation

III. CHOOSING A STRATEGY
Most reasonable now is

To *Rely* on these Church Resources	To *Address* these Ministry Opportunities	To *Offer* these Satisfactions

IV. DEFERRING ACTION
New attention will be deferred on these ministry opportunities and goals:

V. PLANNING FOR IMPLEMENTATION
These programs should be developed:

These groups should be involved:

healthy finances, member loyalty, two different worship services) and column2 the Weaknesses (e.g., low attendance ratio, little visible sharing, few involved in Bible study, few evangelism efforts) of the current church resources of that congregation. Column 3 has Opportunities (e.g., city still growing, many young families, need for day care, few youth activities in the community) and column 4 Threats (e.g., aging membership, many members no longer live in the community) beyond the congregation that present possible needs to be addressed. In consideration of the congregation's resources and of opportunities for ministry, column 5 would be the Satisfactions that can be offered. In business these would be goals to accomplish. The assumption underlying column 5 is that for planning purposes all goals for churches revolve around satisfying some human need apparent within and beyond the fellowship. Certainly offering the spiritual food of Word and Sacraments focused on some specific groups of people would address such satisfaction.

I have done this exercise with a congregation's leaders by giving small groupings a blown-up version of the guide on a 11 x 17 sheet of paper. They quickly get engaged in filling out the columns with enthusiasm.

Doing the five columns is *step one*. The *second step* is to evaluate alternative satisfactions the congregation can offer (e.g., increased youth ministry, more outreach events, specific social services it could offer). This is harder because it defines goals in terms of needs to be satisfied. These are needs in terms of "wants," needs that people know they have and are looking for filling.

Step three is the hardest: choosing one or two outcomes to concentrate on and thus putting the others aside for now. The strategy decision would be to rely on the designated resources to address designated ministry opportunities to accomplish the chosen outcomes.

Then rational planning goes on to determine steps that will be taken to implement that strategy.

This highly rational approach would have been difficult to work out in a congregation, say, a hundred years ago. But we now live in a management culture where such planning is assumed to take place for successful efforts by businesses, social agencies and governments. America's change to a very visible management culture happened in the decades soon after World War II. As developed earlier, better organization was assumed to be the cure for church problems through the 1950s to the 1980s.

FORCE FIELD ANALYSIS

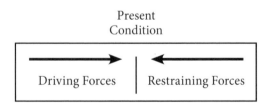

Present
Condition

Driving Forces | Restraining Forces

Social psychologist Kurt Lewin developed a model that is now classic for recognizing the various forces converging on a decision about any transition an organization is considering, as shown in the following graphic.

All the reasons that support making a change to any given condition are represented in the graph as the arrow of Driving Forces. The reasons for not making the change are represented by the arrow of Restraining Forces. When the two arrows are equally matched with driving and restraining forces, there will be no change. Think of the chart as a football field. Those who want change are trying to move the center line to, say, the 30-yard line. When the defense is as strong as the offense, the ball will not be moved. One way to move the ball is by increasing the driving forces. But sometimes this only increases the restraining forces and produces much action and a lot of conflict but no change. A better way with less energy all around is to focus on addressing and reducing the restraining forces.

Imagine a council meeting at First Lutheran Church. Pastor Baumann and some members have come to advocate an alternative worship service. They have experienced such worship at several of the neighboring Lutheran churches. They sincerely think it will increase the number of visitors and then members, and they have gathered demographic material about how many unchurched live within a five-mile radius. The pastor is all for the new service and is willing to put in the extra effort. The proposal is to add an alternative worship service during the Bible class time on Sunday morning.

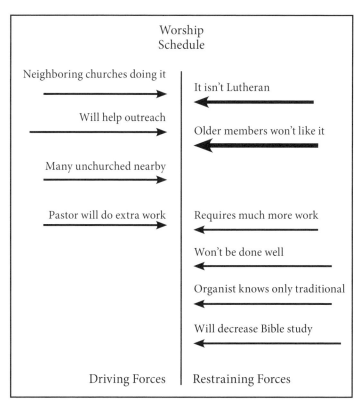

A member of the council, John Mueller, happens to be a management consultant. He suggests taking the time in the meeting to work out a force field analysis. They need especially to concentrate on recognizing the various restraining forces. Their discussion yields the following sketch that Mueller offers:

The reasons not to start an alternative worship service between the early and late services seem significant. Many even on the council consider only hymnal worship to be truly Lutheran. They recall how some of the seniors have made very disparaging comments about a "hootenanny" service that has no place in the sanctuary. The organist has already said she does not know how to do contemporary worship with a praise band. She has in the past commented about how poorly some such services are done. Some of the council members express their worry that doing the alternative service during the Bible study hour will reduce attendance for that.

They conclude there are just too many reasons to keep the schedule the way it is. They encourage the advocates to plan out how they can increase the driving forces and reduce the restraining forces. John Mueller offers to help them think through alternatives.

At the end of the meeting, it would be very important for Pastor Baumann to recognize that proceeding with the proposal as presented would be very unwise. He would be running a huge red light. Conflict is inevitable. Yet this sort of situation unfortunately is a true story for many congregations.

Six months later the advocates for an alternative service come back to the council with a new proposal and the revised force-field analysis that had guided their discussions.

Pastor Baumann reports that he has done research on the Lutheran Confessions on what is considered to be Lutheran worship. Having a variety of formats seems acceptable. The restraining force on that issue has been lessened, as reflected in a shorter and thinner arrow. Since the meeting half a year ago, Pastor Baumann has done much more preaching and talking about mission to others. That line on the importance of mission is shown as longer and thicker. He and others have carried on considerable discussion with individual seniors, as well as their group, and he feels confident that their opposition is lessened, as reflected in a shorter and thinner arrow. A new factor is that an experienced worship leader has been found and is available. This should reduce some of the concern about quality.

The biggest shift, however, came from recognition that resistance to having a worship service during Bible class time has increased, as shown by the longer, thicker line. That red light won't go away. So the advocates now propose to try the new service on Saturday evenings, in line with the success many other churches are reporting.

In response to this discussion, the council approves starting a Saturday evening alternative worship service whenever the group and the new worship leader are ready. They have provided some funds to pay the worship leader part time.

Here is the force-field analysis that guided their planning:

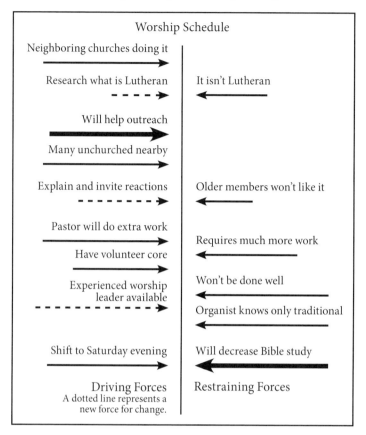

- The resisting force of believing it isn't Lutheran has been considerably reduced (shorter, skinnier line) because of addition of the new force for change of researching what is Lutheran.
- The driving force of "Will help outreach" has been strengthened because of more emphasis in preaching this priority.
- The resisting force of opposition by older members has been reduced by a concerted effort to explain the change to them and to invite their reaction.
- The resisting force of worry about much more work has been reduced by reassurance that the pastor wants to do the extra work and a volunteer core exists.
- The resisting force of concern that the organist knows only traditional and the new may not be well done has been reduced by the additional force of having an experienced worship leader in hand.

- The resisting force of a decrease in Bible study when the contemporary worship is offered at the same time has grown considerably (longer, thicker line). The additional driving force of changing the proposed contemporary service to Saturday evening eliminates that concern.

CONTINUAL TRANSITION

It is humanly natural to assume that whatever transitions are being discussed now will "fix" the problem for the future. But the fundamental problem of today is that the world we live in is changing at an ever-increasing rate. Does anybody really know what our dominant American culture and ways of life will be fifteen years *from now*? What we can know for sure is that there will be no return to the ways of fifteen years *before now*. Technological advancement is irreversible. Greater accessibility to information and ease of connections over the Internet will yield ever-smaller sub-groupings of special interests and probably decrease commitment to past connections.

One alternative is for churches that value their heritage to settle for an ever-smaller niche within the broader society, appealing to a few newcomers who like what they perceive as quaint customs. But I for one would join those church leaders who say this outcome is simply not acceptable.

Better is the alternative to become very clear about what in a church cannot change without being unfaithful to necessary core truths of the Gospel. God does not change, sinful nature does not change, God's promises do not change, what God's Son did on the cross does not change, nor does a final Judgment Day. But how we communicate these truths has indeed changed over the centuries, and for the sake of fruitfulness will undoubtedly have to change in the future.

Faithfulness to their Gospel-driven, outreach-oriented purposes means that healthy congregations will undoubtedly continue to go through more transitions in the years ahead. Church leadership is a process. As the world continues to change around us, so churches need to transition to ways and culture by which we can more fruitfully communicate with those beyond our fellowships.

QUESTIONS FOR DISCUSSION

1. Do you find the distinction between change and transition helpful?

2. How have you viewed the changes in communication technology in recent years? Has your congregation made any transitions?

3. Has your congregation seen a decrease in involvement of young families with children? Why?

4. Have you experienced or witnessed sharp conflict in a congregation over a proposed transition? Could it have been avoided?

5. Have you personally experienced denial and resistance to change going on around you? What might that look like in a congregation?

6. What is your reaction to Reggie McNeal's eight observations about introducing change in churches?

7. Try to find the time to work out a preliminary SWOT-S analysis for your congregation. What strategy would you like to see your church adopt?

8. Pick a transition to change that you would like to see happen, and do a preliminary force field analysis of driving and restraining forces.

9. What is your personal view on how much conflict you can endure in leading a congregation?

10. Share success stories.

Strategic Planning Guide
for _____ Church

I. IDENTIFYING SWOTS

CURRENT CHURCH RESOURCES		POSSIBLE NEEDS TO ADDRESS		POSSIBLE MAJOR GOALS
Strengths	Weaknesses	Opportunities	Threats	Satisfactions to Offer

II. EVALUATING ALTERNATIVES

Importance of Outcomes

Feasibility with resources

Fit with the congregation

III. CHOOSING A STRATEGY
Most reasonable now is

To *Rely* on these Church Resources	To *Address* these Ministry Opportunities	To *Offer* these Satisfactions

IV. DEFERRING ACTION
New attention will be deferred on these ministry opportunities and goals:

V. PLANNING FOR IMPLEMENTATION
These programs should be developed:

These groups should be involved:

CONCLUSION
Working Forward

The discussions of this book have presented contrasting focuses for present-day ministry and church leaders. A superficial reading might see them as opposites: either shepherd or builder, either faithfulness or fruitfulness.

But such simplification does not do justice to the tensions present in those church bodies which intend to spread the Gospel in current American times while honoring their centuries-long traditions fashioned in very different times. The challenge is to sort out the Biblical *truths* that cannot change from the church *practices* that can. The process of modifying church practices to better fit current conditions has been going on for centuries. It will continue so long as the surrounding cultures within which we minister keep evolving, as has been happening at an ever-increasing rate.

The *shepherd* model of ministry and the *builder* model were presented and developed as a way to highlight differing perspectives on how church leaders can and should do ministry in a congregation. They are differing paradigms. The builder model, which in Christian church history actually pre-dates the shepherd model, seems more attuned to the needs in metropolitan areas today. There the desirable conditions of overlap between a church's fellowship and the surrounding social community or parish are disappearing.

Ministry used to assume that a congregation came with a strong sense of community, expressed through many and strong relationships with each other; the need was to guide, counsel, and protect the flock. Now much more attention has to be given first to developing and strengthening the basic community, relationship by relationship. The phrase used here is to "build up fellowship," which was how the Apostle Paul looked at the task for church leaders.

The builder's way highlighted in this book is for leaders to stay focused on helping participants build up their personal relationship with Christ and with each other in their local fellowship of Christ's body. Sharing personal spiritual experiences can serve that purpose well. To be and remain healthy, a Christian congregation needs to keep the focus on its special identity as a spiritual community of believers ever open to how the Holy Spirit shapes them and grows their relationships.

This increased emphasis on experience means that infant-baptizing churches need to move beyond the comfortable and desirable sequence of members who first Belong through baptism, then Believe through confirmation and maybe Experience an awakening later. Where the Spirit seems better able to work in current times is through the sequence of Experience which leads to Belief that leads to Belonging. Helping spiritual experiences happen means to focus more on how the necessary objective truths of Biblical faith become subjective truth in participants' personal faith.

The over-arching theme for these discussions is ministry that needs to be both faithful and fruitful. Like shepherd/builder, it is not *either/or* but *both/and*. Let that relationship be expressed as follows:

Full faithfulness brings lasting fruitfulness.
Lasting fruitfulness depends on full faithfulness.

Two adjectives need to be added to the nouns: *full* faithfulness and *lasting* fruitfulness. *Faithfulness* that leads to withering congregations on the way to dying out is not the faithfulness Jesus and the apostles commend. Lasting *fruitfulness* happens through spiritually transformed lives that see beyond fads and self-interest to share the Gospel persuasively with new people.

Jesus taught that to follow him means to die to self-interests. He said that if you want to save your own life you will lose it; but if you are willing to lose your life for Jesus and the Gospel, you will save it (Mark 8:35). This applies to congregations as well as individuals. Today we might say that ministers and congregations that try to hang on to all their practices and customs of the past may well lose their church, but those who are willing to give up some old practices for the sake of better communicating Biblical truths may well be a lasting fellowship that lives on to minister to a new age. Full faithfulness has to be to the Gospel and the mission of spreading it.

Notes

CHAPTER 1

1. Michael Barone, *Hard America Soft America*, Crown Forum, 2004.
2. www.demographia.com/db-religusa2002.htm.
3. Allan Anderson, *An Introduction to Pentecostalism*, Cambridge University Press, 2004, p. 11.

CHAPTER 3

1. Infoplease at www.infoplease.com/ipa/A0005067.html.
2. The Boston Globe at http://www.boston.com/bostonglobe/editorial_opin ion/oped/articles/2008/02/29/shopping_for_religion/.
3. Robert D. Putnam, *Bowling Alone: The Collapse and Revival of American Community*, Simon and Schuster, 2000.
4. Putnam, *Bowling Alone*, p. 112.
5. Putnam, *Bowling Alone*, p. 68.
6. Putnam, *Bowling Alone*, p. 72.
7. Putnam, *Bowling Alone*, p 76.
8. George Barna, *The Frog in the Kettle: What Christians Need to Know about Life in 2000*. 1990.
9. David S. Luecke, "Trends among Lutheran Preachers," *Word and World*, Volume XIX, Number 1, Winter 1999, pp. 21–29.

CHAPTER 4

1.

Love one another	Romans 13:8
In honor preferring one another	Romans 12:10
Don't judge one another	Romans 14:13
Receive one another	Romans 15:7
Salute one another	Romans 16:16
Greet one another	1 Corinthians 16:20, 2 Corinthians 13:12
Serve one another	Galatians 5:13
Don't provoke or envy one another	Galatians 5:26
Bear one another's burdens	Galatians 5:26
Forbear one another in love	Ephesians 4:2, Colossians 3:13
Forgive one another	Ephesians 4:32, Colossians 3:13
Teach and admonish one another	Colossians 3:16
Comfort one another	1 Thessalonians 4:18
Edify one another	1 Thessalonians 5:11

2. C. F. W. Walther, "Sermon for Day of Repentance, 1870," *Selected Sermons of C. F. W. Walther*, translated by Henry Eggold, Concordia Publishing House, 1981, pp. 155-163.

3. Romans 14:19; 15:2, 20; 1 Corinthians 3:9, 10, 12, 14; 8:1; 14:3, 4, 5, 12, 17; Ephesians 2:20, 21, 22; 4:13, 16, 29; 2 Corinthians 10:8; 12:19; 13:10; 14:26; Colossians 2:7; 1 Thessalonians 5:11; 1 Peter 2:5; Acts 9:31.

4. John Jefferson Davis, "Ephesians 4:12: Once More: 'Equipping the Saints for the Work of Ministry?' " *Evangelical Review of Theology*, 24/2 (2000) pp. 167–176.

5. Gerhard Kittel and Gerhard Friedrich, translated by Geoffrey W. Bromily, *Theological Dictionary of the New Testament: Abridged in One Volume*, Eerdmans, 1985, p. 80.

6. Walter Bauer, Wm. F. Arndt, F. Wilbur Gingrich, and Frederick W. Danker, *A Greek-English Lexicon of the New Testament*, 2nd edition, University of Chicago Press, 1958, p. 418.

CHAPTER 5

1. Robert W. Schaibley, "Lutheran Preaching: Proclamation, Not Communication," *Concordia Journal*, January 1992, pp 6–25.

2. Schaibley, p. 9.

3. Schaibley, p. 20.

4. David S. Luecke, "Trends among Lutheran Preachers," *Word and World*, Winter 1999.

5. David S. Luecke, *Apostolic Style and Lutheran Substance: Ten Years of Controversy over What Can Change*, Fairway Press, 1999, p. 82.

6. James F. White, *Protestant Worship: Traditions in Transition*, Westminster/John Knox, 1989, p. 42.

7. James Alan Waddell, *The Struggle to Reclaim the Liturgy in the Lutheran Church: Adiaphora in Historical, Theological and Practical Perspective*, The Edwin Mellen Press, 2005, p. 274.

8. David S. Luecke, *How Much to Pray for Healing?* Fairway Press, 2004.

9. Luecke, cited above, p. 9.

10. Alister E. McGrath, *Christian Spirituality*, 1999, p. 2.

CHAPTER 6

1. David S. Luecke and Samuel Southard, *Pastoral Administration: Integrating Ministry and Management in the Church*, Word, 1986.

2. Richard G. Hutcheson, Jr. *Wheel Within the Wheel*, John Knox Press, 1979.

3. Avery Dulles, *Models of the Church*, 1974, 2002.

4. Martin Luther, *Small Catechism*, Explanation to the Third Article.

5. Martin Luther, *The Large Catechism*, paragraph 43.

6. Smalcald Articles, Part III, Article IV.

7. Smalcald Articles, Part III, Article IV.

CHAPTER 7

1. *Handbook of Religious Experience*, ed. Ralph W. Hood, Religious Education Press, 1995.
   Andre Godin, *The Psychological Dynamics of Religious Experience*, Religious Education Press, 1985.
   H. Newton Malony, *Psychology of Religion*, Baker, 1991.
   Benedict J. Groeschel, *Spiritual Passages: The Psychology of Spiritual Development*, Crossroads, 1995.
2. Charles Glock and Rodney Stark, *Religion and Society in Tension*, quoted in Margaret M. Poloma, "The Sociological Context of Religious Experience," in *Handbook of Religious Experience*, ed. Ralph W. Hood, Religious Education Press, 1995, p. 169.
3. Rudolf Otto, *The Idea of the Holy*, translated by J. W. Harvey Oxford University Press, (1917), 1950.
4. Poloma, cited above, p. 171.
5. Poloma, cited above, p. 171.
6. David S. Luecke, *Talking with God: How Ordinary Christians Grow in Prayer*, Fellowship Ministries, 1997, p. 60.
7. H. Newton Maloney, "Conversion: The Sociodynamics of Change," in *Psychology of Religion*, ed. H. Newton Malony, Baker, 1991, p. 203.
8. Jamet P. Hagberg and Robert A. Guelich, *The Critical Journey: Stages in the Life of Faith*, 1995.
9. Charles Keating, *Who We Are Is How We Pray*, 1987.
   Chester P. Michael and Marie C. Norrisey, *Prayer and Temperament: Different Prayer Forms for Different Personality Types*, 1991.
10. William Hordern, *Experience and Faith*, Augsburg, 1983, p. 98.
11. Matthew A. Elliott, *Faithful Feelings: Rethinking Emotion in the New Testament*, Kregel, 2006, pp. 18–52.
12. Elliott, cited above, p. 54.
13. Elliott, p. 143.
14. Anthony B. Robinson, *Transforming Congregational Culture*, Baker, 2003, p. 40.

CHAPTER 8

1. Wikipedia (http://en.widipedia.org/wiki/Organizational_culture)
2. Janet Letnes Martin and Suzann (Johnson) Nelson, *Growing Up Lutheran: What Does This Mean?* Caragana Press, 1997.
3. William D'Antonio, Dean Hoge, James Davidson, and Mary Gautier, *American Catholics Today: New Realities of Their Faith and Their Church*, Roman and Littlefield, 2007.
4. Brian Mockenhaupt, "The Army We Have," *The Atlantic Monthly*, June 2007.

5. "Language Question in the Lutheran Church (U.S.)," *Lutheran Cyclopedia*, Concordia Publishing House, 1954, p. 568.
6. David S. Luecke, *The Other Story of Lutherans at Worship: Reclaiming Our Heritage of Diversity*, Fellowship Ministries, 1995, p. 81.
7. Thomas Schattauer, "A Liturgical Prospect," his third presentation at the Convocation of Luther Seminary of St. Paul, Minnesota, in January 1996.
8. David S. Luecke, *Talking with God: How Ordinary Christians Grow in Prayer*, Fellowship Ministries, 1997.
9. King of Kings Lutheran Church, Omaha, Nebraska, 1999.
10. Formula of Concord, Solid Declaration, Article X, paragraph 9.
11. David S. Luecke, *Evangelical Style and Lutheran Substance*, Concordia Publishing House, 1988.
12. Richard John Neuhaus, "What's Really Wrong with the Church Growth Movement: The Lutheran Difference," *Lutheran Forum*, August 1990.

CHAPTER 9

1. Douglas W. Johnson, *The Care and Feeding of Volunteers*, Abingdon, 1978.
2. Douglas W. Johnson, *Empowering Lay Volunteers*, Abingdon 1991.
3. Avery Dulles, *Models of the Church*, 1974, 2002.
4. Christian A. Schwarz, *Natural Church Development: A Guide to Eight Essential Qualities of Healthy Churches*, Church Smart Resources, 1998, p. 18.
5. Schwarz, cited above, p. 40.
6. Win Arn, Carroll Nyquist, and Charles Arn, *Who Cares about Love?* Church Growth Press, 1986, pp. 118, 129.
7. Aubrey Malphurs, *Values-Driven Leadership: Discovering and Developing Your Core Values for Ministry*, 1996; *Developing a Dynamic Mission for Your Ministry: Finding Direction and Making an Impact as a Church Leader*, 1998.
8. John Carver, *Boards That Make a Difference: A New Design for Leadership in Nonprofit and Public Organizations*, 1990; *Reinventing Your Board: A Step-By-Step Guide to Implementing Policy Governance*, 1997.
9. Christian A. Schwarz, *Paradigm Shift in the Church: How Natural Church Development Can Transform Theological Thinking*, Church Smart Resources, 1999.
10. Emil Brunner, *Truth as Encounter*, Westminster Press, 1964, p. 77.

CHAPTER 10

1. Paul Hersey, Ken Blanchard, *Management of Organizational Behavior* (9th edition), 2007.
2. Hersey and Blanchard, *The One Minute Manage* (10th edition), 2000.
3. As further developed in David S. Luecke and Samuel Southard, *Pastoral Administration*, Word Publishing, 1986, chapter 7.

4. *Concordia Study Bible*, ed. Robert G. Hoerber, undated, pp. 1674–1675.

CHAPTER 11

1. William Bridges, *Managing Transitions*, Perseus Books, 2003, p. 3.
2. Gary Thies, Mission Development Counselor, Iowa West District of The Lutheran Church—Missouri Synod, gary.thies@lcms.org.
3. Cynthia D. Scott and Dennis T. Jaffe, *Managing Organizational Change*, Crisp Publications, 1989.
4. Scott and Jaffe, p. 33.
5. Reggie McNeal, Module 3, "Managing Changing and Transition," *Developing Leaders for Ministry*, a project of The Lutheran Church—Missouri Synod, 1995.
6. McNeal, as cited above.
7. McNeal, as cited above.
8. McNeal, as cited above.
9. McNeal, Module 2, "Creating an Innovative Congregational Culture," *Developing Leaders for Ministry*, a project of The Lutheran Church—Missouri Synod, 1995.